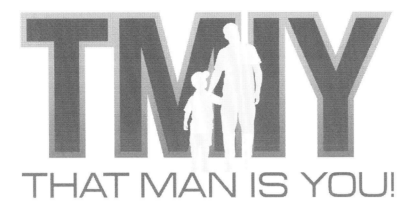

THY KINGDOM COME

PowerPoint Presentations

Paradisus Dei

HELPING FAMILIES DISCOVER THE SUPERABUNDANCE OF GOD

A Publication of Paradisus Dei • www.paradisusdei.org

Thy Kingdom Come

Capuchin Crypt

> As you are now, we once were.
> As we are now, you shall be.

Memento Mori

> Remember your last days and set enmity aside; remember death and decay, and cease from sin!
>
> - Sirach 28:6

Eternal Perspective: Life is Short

> What is your life? For you are a mist that appears for a little time and then vanishes.
>
> - James 4:14

The Kingdom of God and Death

> Then comes the end, when he delivers the kingdom to God the Father after destroying every rule and every authority and power. For he must reign until he has put all his enemies under his feet. The last enemy to be destroyed is death.
>
> - 1 Corinthians 15:24-26

Triumph Over Death

> O death, where is thy victory? O death, where is thy sting?
>
> — 1 Corinthians 15:55

TMIY

Perspective on Fear

> And do not fear those who kill the body but cannot kill the soul; rather fear him who can destroy both soul and body in hell.
>
> — Matthew 10:28

TMIY

Living for the Kingdom

Christian Charity
The Golden Rule: Do unto Others
Sacrificial Love: As Christ Loved
No Greater Love: Lay Down Life

Evangelical Boldness
Woe to me if I do not preach the gospel!
Go Make Disciples of All Nations
Seek First the Kingdom of God

Eternal Perspective

Fear
O Death Where is Thy Victory
Do Not Fear Those Who Can Kill the Body
Fear Him Who Can Destroy Soul and Body

Prudence
Mother of All Virtues
Not Good for Man to be Alone
Devoted to the Fellowship

TMIY

The Providence of God

And he said to his disciples, "Therefore I tell you, do not be anxious about your life, what you shall eat, nor about your body, what you shall put on. For life is more than food, and the body more than clothing. Consider the ravens: they neither sow nor reap, they have neither storehouse nor barn, and yet God feeds them. Of how much more value are you than the birds! And which of you by being anxious can add a cubit to his span of life?If then you are not able to do as small a thing as that, why are you anxious about the rest?

- Luke 12: 22-26

The Providence of God

Consider the lilies, how they grow; they neither toil nor spin; yet I tell you, even Solomon in all his glory was not arrayed like one of these. But if God so clothes the grass which is alive in the field today and tomorrow is thrown into the oven, how much more will he clothe you, O men of little faith! And do not seek what you are to eat and what you are to drink, nor be of anxious mind. For all the nations of the world seek these things; and your Father knows that you need them. Instead, seek his kingdom, and these things shall be yours as well.

- Luke 12: 27-31

The Father's Pleasure

Fear not, little flock, for it is your Father's good pleasure to give you the kingdom. Sell your possessions, and give alms; provide yourselves with purses that do not grow old, with a treasure in the heavens that does not fail, where no thief approaches and no moth destroys. For where your treasure is, there will your heart be also.

- Luke 12: 32-34

The 7 Steps of That Man Is You!

1. Honor your wedding vows
2. Use money for others
3. Give God some of your time
4. Set your mind on things above
5. Find God in yourself
6. Find God in other people
7. Practice Superabundant Mercy

TMIY

A Time for Purification

" I consider that the sufferings of this present time are not worth comparing with the glory that is to be revealed to us.

- Romans 8:18 "

TMIY

 Session 1

- In this tension between gravity and grace, what efforts do you take to "Set Your Mind on the Things Above?" Do you desire to have an "Eternal Perspective" like the saints?

- Which terrifies you more? Fear of death or fear of sin? What can you do to avoid sin in your life and help others avoid sin?

Session 02

The Kingdom is Like Leaven

Called to Serve

> The Son of man came not to be served but to serve.
>
> -Matthew 20:28

TMIY

The Parable of the Yeast

> He told them another parable. "The kingdom of heaven is like leaven which a woman took and hid in three measures of flour, till it was all leavened.
>
> -Matthew 13:33

TMIY

To Give Thanks

Eucharisteo
To give thanks, to be grateful, to return thanks

Superabundance

Being Catholic
We have more feast days than fast days.

The Greatest Commandment

Love one another; even as I have loved you, that you also love one another.

-John 13:34

The Fire of Discipline

> Discipline your son, and he will give you rest; he will give delight to your heart.
>
> -Proverbs 29:17

Salt and Light

> You are the salt of the earth...
> You are the light of the world.
>
> -Matthew 5:13-14

Know Your Children

Temperament
You have to know the temperament and temperature that your children can handle when it comes to you disciplining them.

Every one of us is unique.

TMIY

Brioche Monte Cristo with a Flambéed Berry Compote and Whipped Cream

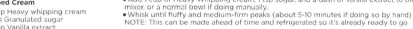

Ingredients:

Sandwich
- 1 Loaf or package of brioche bread
- 3 Large eggs
- 1 Cup Half and Half
- ¼ Cup Dark Brown Sugar
- 1 tsp Ground Nutmeg
- 2 tsp Ground Cinnamon
- 1 tsp Vanilla Extract
- 6 Tbs Butter
- 1 Package of sliced ham
- 1 Small wedge/package of brie cheese
- 1 Box panko breadcrumbs
- 1 Box Italian seasoned breadcrumbs

Mixed Berry Compote
- 1 Container Strawberries sliced (apx ½ cup of sliced strawberries)
- 1 Container Blackberries (apx ½ cup of blackberries)
- 1 Container Raspberries
- 3 Tbs Dark rum
- 2 Tbs Butter
- 1 Pinch of Salt (optional)
- 1 tsp Granulated sugar (optional)

Whipped Cream
- 1 Cup Heavy whipping cream
- 1 tsp Granulated sugar
- ¼ tsp Vanilla extract

Instructions:

Sandwich
- Combine eggs, half and half, brown sugar, nutmeg, cinnamon, and vanilla extract in a bowl and whisk until combined.
- Combine equal parts panko breadcrumbs and Italian seasoned breadcrumbs in a separate bowl.
- If using Brioche rolls slice in half; if using a whole loaf slice in 1-inch thick slices; if using pre-cut bread, you can skip this step.
- Take a fork and poke holes in your bread about every inch to help it absorb the custard. Then assemble the sandwich with a few slices of ham and brie cheese.
- Submerge the sandwich into the custard, followed by the panko breadcrumb mix, making sure to get an even coating of breadcrumbs on the outside.
- Add 6 Tbs of butter to a pan on medium-high heat and let brown. When brown carefully add the sandwiches to the pan.
- Cook sandwiches until nice and golden brown on the outside and the cheese is nice and melted in the center (roughly 6-8 minutes) flipping halfway. Remove from heat when done and enjoy.

Mixed Berry Compote
- Add the remaining 2 Tbs of butter to a pan on medium-high heat and let brown.
- When brown, add black berries to the pan and sauté on high.
- Turn off the heat and add 2-3 Tbs of rum to the pan. After the rum is added turn the flame back on high and tilt the pan slightly to allow the flame to come in contact with the rum to flambe.
- After the flame has died out, add the sliced strawberries to the pan and toss, then turn off the heat so they don't become mushy.
- Add a tsp of sugar (optional) and a pinch of salt to the berries.
- Add the raspberries to the pan and toss right before serving as they are the most delicate.

Whipped Cream
- Add 1 cup of Heavy Whipping cream, 1 tsp sugar, and a dash of vanilla extract to the bowl of a stand mixer, or a normal bowl if doing manually.
- Whisk until fluffy and medium-firm peaks (about 5-10 minutes if doing so by hand)
NOTE: This can be made ahead of time and refrigerated so it's already ready to go.

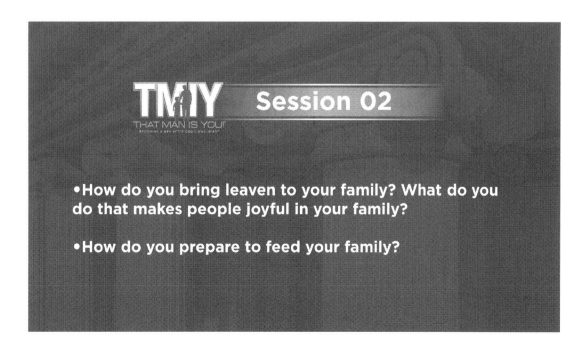

TMIY THAT MAN IS YOU — **Session 02**

- **How do you bring leaven to your family? What do you do that makes people joyful in your family?**

- **How do you prepare to feed your family?**

Session 03

Christ the King

The Kingdom of God

Behold, the kingdom of God
is in your midst.

-Luke 17:21

TMIY

A World of Grave Difficulties

It is necessary, then, to keep a watchful eye on this our world, with its problems and values, its unrest and hopes, its defeats and triumphs: a world whose economic, social, political and cultural affairs pose problems and grave difficulties...

-Christifideles Laici

TMIY

The World Today

> We are no longer under a Christian regime because the faith—especially in Europe, but also in much of the West—no longer constitutes an obvious premise of common life. On the contrary, it is even often denied, derided, marginalized and ridiculed.
>
> -Pope Francis

TMIY

A Post Christian World

1	Rejection of God
2	
3	

TMIY

A Post Christian World

1	Rejection of God
2	Feelings Determine Truth - Feelings are Facts
3	

TMIY

A Post Christian World

1 Rejection of God

2 Feelings Determine Truth - Feelings are Facts

3 Freedom is doing whatever the individual wants

A Pre-Christian World

1 A New/Chosen Identity

5

2

6

3

7

4

8

Clothed in Christ

For in Christ Jesus you are all sons of God, through faith. For as many of you as were baptized into Christ have put on Christ. There is neither Jew nor Greek, there is neither slave nor free, there is neither male nor female; for you are all one in Christ Jesus.

-Galatians 3:26-28

A Pre-Christian World

1	A New/Chosen Identity	5	
2	Christ at Center of Everything	6	
3		7	
4		8	

TMIY

Not a Political Movement

> " But we preach Christ crucified, a stumbling block to Jews and folly to Gentiles, but to those who are called, both Jews and Greeks, Christ the power of God and the wisdom of God.
>
> -1 Corinthians 1:23-24 "

TMIY

Freedom

> " For freedom Christ has set us free.
>
> -Galations 5:1 "

TMIY

A Pre-Christian World

1 A New/Chosen Identity		**5**	
2 Christ at Center of Everything		**6**	
3 Loved their Enemies		**7**	
4		**8**	

TMIY

A Pre-Christian World

1 A New/Chosen Identity		**5**	
2 Christ at Center of Everything		**6**	
3 Loved their Enemies		**7**	
4 Hospitality to Poor/Despised		**8**	

TMIY

For the Least of My People

66

For I was hungry and you gave me food, I was thirsty and you gave me drink, I was a stranger and you welcomed me, I was naked and you clothed me, I was sick and you visited me, I was in prison and you came to me.

-Matthew 25:35-36 99

TMIY

A Pre-Christian World

1 A New/Chosen Identity		**5** Counter Cultural	
2 Christ at Center of Everything		**6**	
3 Loved their Enemies		**7**	
4 Hospitality to Poor/ Despised		**8**	

TMIY

A Pre-Christian World

1 A New/Chosen Identity		**5** Counter Cultural	
2 Christ at Center of Everything		**6** Communal	
3 Loved their Enemies		**7**	
4 Hospitality to Poor/ Despised		**8**	

TMIY

A Community of Believers

And day by day, attending the temple together and breaking bread in their homes, they partook of food with glad and generous hearts, praising God and having favor with all the people.

-Acts 2:46-47 "

TMIY

A Pre-Christian World

1	A New/Chosen Identity		**5**	Counter Cultural
2	Christ at Center of Everything		**6**	Communal
3	Loved their Enemies		**7**	Worship
4	Hospitality to Poor/ Despised		**8**	

TMIY

A Pre-Christian World

1	A New/Chosen Identity		**5**	Counter Cultural
2	Christ at Center of Everything		**6**	Communal
3	Loved their Enemies		**7**	Worship
4	Hospitality to Poor/ Despised		**8**	Eternal Perspective

TMIY

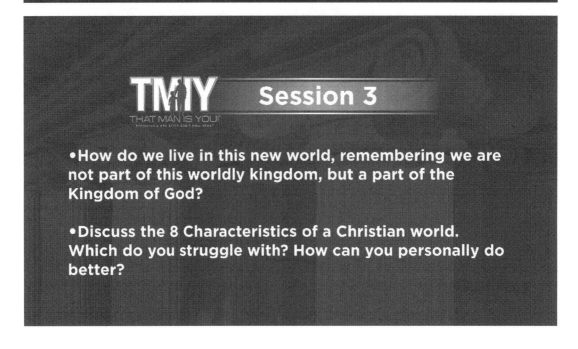

TMIY
THAT MAN IS YOU!

Session 3

- **How do we live in this new world, remembering we are not part of this worldly kingdom, but a part of the Kingdom of God?**

- **Discuss the 8 Characteristics of a Christian world. Which do you struggle with? How can you personally do better?**

Session 04

The Overthrow of Satan

The Kingdom of God

> Repent, for the kingdom of heaven is at hand.
>
> -Matthew 4:17

TMIY

Things are About to Change

> And Jesus, full of the Holy Spirit, returned from the Jordan, and was led by the Spirit for forty days in the wilderness, tempted by the devil.
>
> -Luke 4:1-2

TMIY

The Battle is Being Waged

> The coming of God's kingdom means the defeat of Satan's: "If it is by the Spirit of God that I cast out demons, then the kingdom of God has come upon you."
>
> -CCC 550

The evil one

> If any faint suspicion of your existence begins to arise in his mind, suggest to him a picture of something in red tights, and persuade him that since he cannot believe in that (it is an old textbook method of confusing them) he therefore cannot believe in you.
>
> -CS Lewis

The Two Kingdoms

Jesus ushers in the Kingdom of God but the two kingdoms are profoundly opposed to each other.

The Three Obstacles in the Spiritual Life

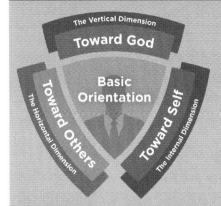

The Devil	"The pride of life."
The World	"The concupiscence of the eyes."
The Flesh	"The concupiscence of the flesh."

TMIY

The Consequences of Original Sin

The consequences of original sin and of all men's personal sins put the world as a whole in the sinful condition aptly described in St. John's expression, "the sin of the world.

-CCC 408

TMIY

The Power of Satan

The power of Satan is, nonetheless, not infinite. He is only a creature, powerful from the fact that he is pure spirit, but still a creature. He cannot prevent the building up of God's reign.

-CCC 395

TMIY

•How do you experience the power of the world? What is your greatest temptation and greatest struggle?

•Are you able to make a distinction between the kingdom of the world and the Kingdom of God? Describe an experience when the Kingdom of God triumphed over sin in your life.

Session 05

How to Overthrow An Empire

How to Overthrow an Empire

Self-Sacrificial Generosity as
Apostolic Evangelization

Called Himself the King

" When the Son of man comes in his glory, and all the angels with him, then he will sit on his glorious throne. Before him will be gathered all the nations, and he will separate them one from another as a shepherd separates the sheep from the goats, and he will place the sheep at his right hand, but the goats at the left. Then the King will say to those at his right hand, 'Come, O blessed of my Father, inherit the kingdom prepared for you from the foundation of the world.'

-Matthew 25:31-34 "

Publicly Confirmed

"Are you the King of the Jews?" ... Jesus answered, "My kingship is not of this world; if my kingship were of this world, my servants would fight, that I might not be handed over to the Jews; but my kingship is not from the world."

-John 18:33-36

TMIY

Proclaimed It

All authority in heaven and on earth has been given to me. Go therefore and make disciples of all nations, baptizing them in the name of the Father and of the Son and of the Holy Spirit, teaching them to observe all that I have commanded you; and lo, I am with you always, to the close of the age.

-Matthew 28:18-20

TMIY

Universal, Moral and Spiritual

1 How Does the Kingdom Grow?

TMIY

Universal, Moral and Spiritual

1	How Does the Kingdom Grow?
2	Who Enters the Kingdom?

TMIY

Universal, Moral and Spiritual

1	How Does the Kingdom Grow?
2	Who Enters the Kingdom?
3	Who Opposes the Kingdom?

TMIY

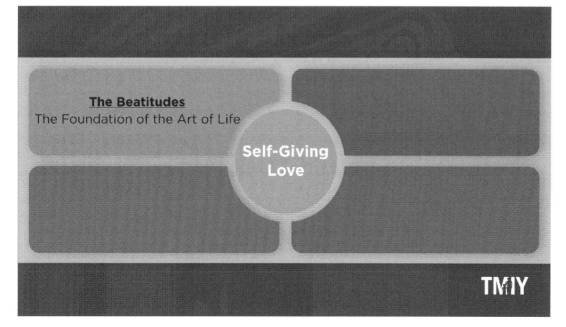

The Beatitudes
The Foundation of the Art of Life

Self-Giving
Love

TMIY

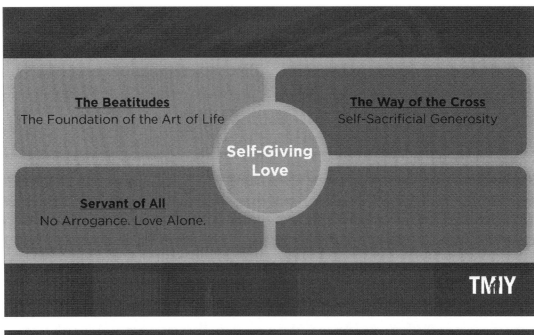
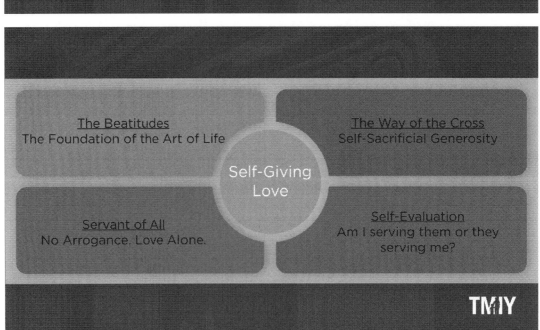

How to Overthrow an Empire

- •Am I serving others (spouse, children, co-workers, friends) or are they serving me?

- •How can I concretely serve others with a greater generosity?

Session 06

Word - Witness - Walk

Word - Witness - Walk

Sanctity Preaches Louder Than Words

 TMIY

Divine Power Through His Word

" In the beginning God created the heavens and the earth. The earth was without form and void, and darkness was upon the face of the deep; and the Spirit of God was moving over the face of the waters.
And God said, "Let there be light"; and there was light.

-Genesis 1:1-3 "

 TMIY

Word - Witness - Walk

Word ▶ The Word was Made Flesh so that You can Follow Him!

▶

▶

A New Creation Story

> In the beginning was the Word, and the Word was with God, and the Word was God ... And the Word became flesh and dwelt among us.
>
> -John 1:1-14

Word - Witness - Walk

Word ▶ The Word was Made Flesh so that You can Follow Him!

Witness ▶ Before You Preach or Teach, Get Your House in Order!

▶

Word - Witness - Walk

Word	The Word was Made Flesh so that You can Follow Him!
Witness	Before You Preach or Teach, Get Your House in Order!
Walk	Let Your Light Shine Before Men that They Glorify God!

TMIY

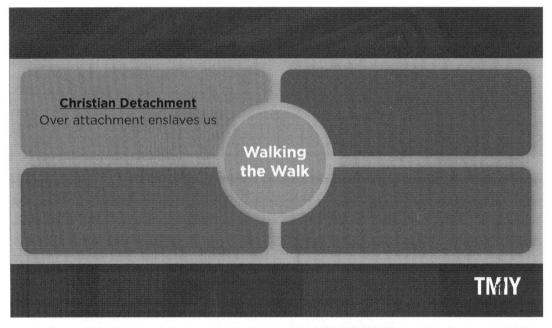

Christian Detachment
Over attachment enslaves us

Walking the Walk

TMIY

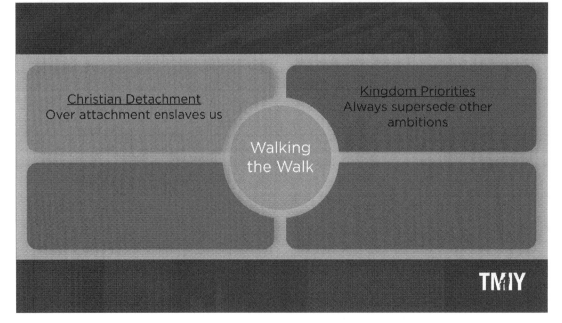

Christian Detachment
Over attachment enslaves us

Kingdom Priorities
Always supersede other ambitions

Walking the Walk

TMIY

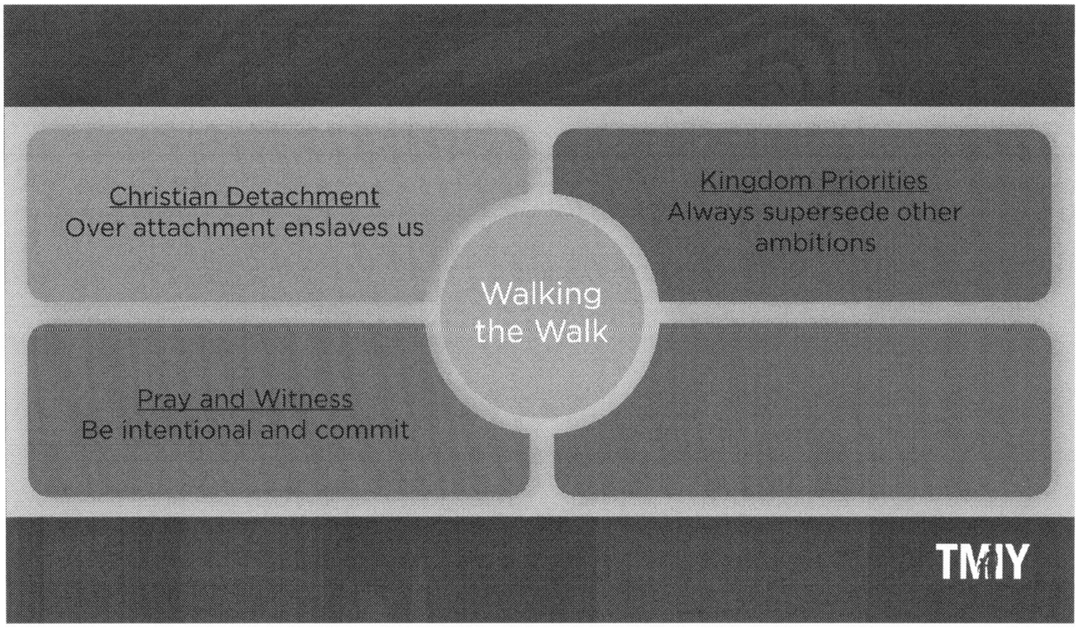
Christian Detachment
Over attachment enslaves us
Kingdom Priorities
Always supersede other ambitions
Walking the Walk
Pray and Witness
Be intentional and commit
TMIY

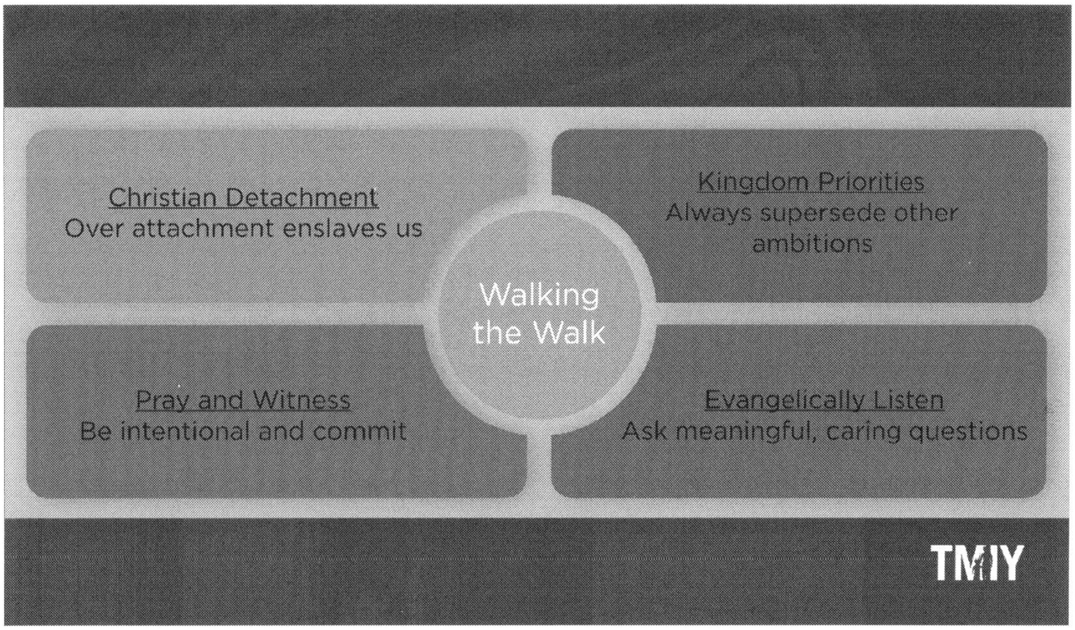
Christian Detachment
Over attachment enslaves us
Kingdom Priorities
Always supersede other ambitions
Walking the Walk
Pray and Witness
Be intentional and commit
Evangelically Listen
Ask meaningful, caring questions
TMIY

Christian Detachment
Over attachment enslaves us
Kingdom Priorities
Always supersede other ambitions
Walking the Walk
Pray and Witness
Be intentional and commit
Evangelically Listen
Ask meaningful, caring questions
Be Active in Your Evangelization!
TMIY

Session 06

• Have I ever explicitly shared the Gospel with another person in word and action? If not, what are the obstacles holding you back?

• Be concrete. Share the name of one person in your life who needs Christ. Why do you feel this way? Commit to praying for this person daily. Ask God for the opportunity to share the Gospel with this person.

Session 07

The Men We Need
To Build the Kingdom

The Centerpiece

The centerpiece of a holy priest's vocation is an identification with the crucified Christ.

TMIY

Eight Characteristics of Holy Men

1	Adoration of the Eucharistic Face of Jesus	5	
2		6	
3		7	
4		8	

TMIY

Eight Characteristics of Holy Men

#		#	
1	Adoration of the Eucharistic Face of Jesus	5	
2	Devotion to Our Blessed Mother	6	
3		7	
4		8	

TMIY

Eight Characteristics of Holy Men

#		#	
1	Adoration of the Eucharistic Face of Jesus	5	
2	Devotion to Our Blessed Mother	6	
3	A Devoted Prayer Life	7	
4		8	

TMIY

Eight Characteristics of Holy Men

#		#	
1	Adoration of the Eucharistic Face of Jesus	5	
2	Devotion to Our Blessed Mother	6	
3	A Devoted Prayer Life	7	
4	A Spirit of Asceticism	8	

TMIY

Eight Characteristics of Holy Men

1	Adoration of the Eucharistic Face of Jesus	**5**	Demands of Fatherhood
2	Devotion to Our Blessed Mother	**6**	
3	A Devoted Prayer Life	**7**	
4	A Spirit of Asceticism	**8**	

TMIY

Eight Characteristics of Holy Men

1	Adoration of the Eucharistic Face of Jesus	**5**	Demands of Fatherhood
2	Devotion to Our Blessed Mother	**6**	Carpe Diem Mentality of Diving into Travailed Souls
3	A Devoted Prayer Life	**7**	
4	A Spirit of Asceticism	**8**	

TMIY

Eight Characteristics of Holy Men

1	Adoration of the Eucharistic Face of Jesus	**5**	Demands of Fatherhood
2	Devotion to Our Blessed Mother	**6**	Carpe Diem Mentality of Diving into Travailed Souls
3	A Devoted Prayer Life	**7**	The Prophetic Voice
4	A Spirit of Asceticism	**8**	

TMIY

Eight Characteristics of Holy Men

1 Adoration of the Eucharistic Face of Jesus

2 Devotion to Our Blessed Mother

3 A Devoted Prayer Life

4 A Spirit of Asceticism

5 Demands of Fatherhood

6 Carpe Diem Mentality of Diving into Travailed Souls

7 The Prophetic Voice

8 Available for Family 24/7

TMIY

Suffering Saints

I understood that I must lead Christ's Church into this third millennium through suffering ... Precisely because the family is threatened, the family is under attack. The Pope has to be attacked, the Pope has to suffer, so that every family and the world may see that there is ... a higher Gospel ... by which the future is prepared, the third millennium of families.

- Pope St. John Paul II

TMIY

The Cross

If any man would come after me, let him deny himself and take up his cross and follow me. For whoever would save his life will lose it, and whoever loses his life for my sake will find it.

-Matthew 14:24-25

TMIY

• What are examples or ways you can embrace and incorporate "small martyrdoms" into your daily life? How will embracing "small martyrdoms" help as you move forward in time?

• As you listened to the proposed Eight Characteristics of Holy Priests and Men, did any jump out to nudge you toward greater participation? Of the proposed Eight Characteristics of Holy Priests and Men, which do you consider the most vital for this time? Can they even be ranked in priority?

Session 08

The Kingdom of Comfort

On Poverty

A life of real poverty, Gospel poverty such as Jesus lived, is not comfortable. It is not pleasant. It is not easy. It is painful. This is the life Jesus lived. ... Christ freely chose poverty. He chose extreme, excessive, radical poverty. Christ by deliberate choice was born poor, He lived poor, and he died poor in order to give us an example.

-Fr. Aloysius Schwartz

TMIY

Apparition at Banneux

"I come to relieve suffering." This is an echo of the words of Jesus in the Gospel. I come to serve. I have not come to be served, but to serve, to relieve suffering, especially that of the poor."

Our Lady at Banneux

TMIY

A Letter by Fr. Aloysius

To the Virgin of the Poor:
For a long time now I have entrusted to you all that I have & all that
I am. You have taken all, I have nothing. I am poor.
My health you have taken.
My good name you have taken. I am now counted among the disobedient or psychotics or fools. I do not think I exaggerate.
My country (Korea) you have torn from me.
My mission vocation seems to be lost.
My friends for the most part leave me to my own devices.
Materially I have little.

Dec 31, 1958
Kyoto, Japan

A Letter by Fr. Aloysius

O Virgin of the Poor, I thank you.
I wanted poverty, and it embraces me fiercely.
Virgin, no, I give you nothing. You have given me the gift of poverty and suffering & by these two pearls I am ground into a host.

O Mary, I dare not say I have nothing more to give or what remains (I do not know). Will it be torn from me as a limb?
But I renew—so deeply conscious of what I am, my weakness, my imperfection—the words of consecration: all I have and am—all!

Dec 31, 1958
Kyoto, Japan

A Letter by Fr. Aloysius

Virgin of the Poor, yes!
But O Mother, have pity,
I am a beggar and alone, and I am so weary.
But I will risk all.

O Virgin of the Poor, have pity on me. Look at my tears, have pity, have pity, have pity.

-Aloysius Schwartz
Priest and Beggar

Dec 31, 1958
Kyoto, Japan

The Sisters of Mary

We come to save souls. In a sense, we come to purchase souls for God. These are old-fashioned words but they are traditional and are very much in harmony with Jesus. But the price of an immortal soul is blood. ... Our role is to mingle our blood with the blood of Christ and to shed our blood with that of Christ to the poor. The way we serve is to have a constant crown of thorns.

-The Sisters of Mary

The Sisters of Mary

Time for us here is like Magdalene's perfume. It is precious to us. We give everything to them. The children have been through too much.

-A Sister of Mary

To Be Fully Given

To live poverty means that I must accept a certain death. Now, it is not easy for me, but I know I need to die several times a day. I need to leave behind everything that I am. But that is the Gospel—I leave everything—mother, father, all that I have. This is what Jesus asks. It is difficult, but these difficulties are great gifts. Because they allow me to offer myself fully to Him and these girls.

-Sr. Marinae in Chalco, Mexico

Session 08

•The Sisters' witness is to die to self each day to resurrect broken souls; their sacrificial act of love is helping to save the Church. What are ways you can die to yourself to help those you know are suffering?

•Fr. Al knew that he had to be poor to truly help the poor. What does this mean? Are there places you can eliminate comforts and luxuries in your life to live more like Christ in his stark poverty?

Session 09

Acquiring A Taste For Heaven

Heaven and This World

Heaven then is not like this world; I will say what it is much more like – a church. For in a place of public worship no language of this world is heard; there are no schemes brought forward for temporal objects, great or small; no information how to strengthen our worldly interests, extend our influence, or establish our credit. These things indeed may be right in their own way, provided we do not set our hearts upon them; still (I repeat), it is certain that we hear nothing of them in a church...

TMIY

Heaven and This World

Here we hear solely and entirely of God. We praise Him, worship Him, sing to Him, thank Him, confess to Him, give ourselves up to Him, and ask His blessing.

And therefore, a church is like heaven; namely, because both in the one and the other, there is one sovereign subject – religion – brought before us.

St. John Henry Newman,
Holiness Necessary for Future Blessedness

TMIY

Heaven for the Unholy

Supposing a man of unholy life were suffered to enter Heaven, he would not be happy there; so it would be no mercy to permit him to enter.

St. John Henry Newman,
Holiness Necessary for Future Blessedness

TMIY

Heaven Is Real

Reality is harsh to the feet of shadows.

C. S. Lewis,
The Great Divorce

TMIY

The Rich Young Man

And as he was setting out on his journey, a man ran up and knelt before him, and asked him, "Good Teacher, what must I do to inherit eternal life?" And Jesus said to him, "Why do you call me good? No one is good but God alone. You know the commandments. 'Do not kill, Do not commit adultery, Do not bear false witness, Do not defraud, Honor your father and mother, Love your neighbor as yourself.'" And he said to Jesus, "Teacher, all these I have observed from my youth."

Mark 10:17-21

TMIY

The Rich Young Man

> And Jesus looking upon him loved him, and said to him, "You lack one thing; go, sell what you have, and give to the poor, and you will have treasure in heaven; and come, follow me." At that saying [the man's] countenance fell, and he went away sorrowful; for he had great possessions.

Mark 10:121–22

The Rich Man and Lazarus

> There was a rich man who was clothed in purple and fine linen and who feasted sumptuously every day. And at his gate lay a poor man named Lazarus, full of sores, who desired to be fed with what fell from the rich man's table; moreover dogs came and licked his sores. The poor man died and was carried by angels to Abraham's bosom. The rich man died also and was buried; and in Hades, being in torment, he lifted up his eyes, and saw Abraham far off and Lazarus in his bosom.

Luke 16:19–28

The Rich Young Man

> And he called out, "Father Abraham, have mercy upon me, and send Lazarus to dip the end of his finger in water and cool my tongue; for I am in anguish in this flame." But Abraham said, "Son, remember that you in your lifetime received your good things, and Lazarus in like manner evil things; but now he is comforted and you are in anguish. And besides all this, between us and you a great chasm has been fixed..."

Luke 16:19–28

Session 09

- The Rich Young Man resented the way Christ called him to eternal life. What is a call or a sacrifice you currently fear or might fear?

- How does the shift from thinking about "getting in to Heaven" to "loving Heaven" change the way you see or think about salvation?

Session 10

Blinded By The Kingdom

Introduction to Paul

> Saul was trying to destroy the church; entering house after house and dragging out men and women, he handed them over for imprisonment.
>
> Acts 8:3

TMIY

Paul's Memory of Who He Was

> I am a Jew, born in Tarsus in Cilicia, but brought up in this city. At the feet of Gamaliel I was educated strictly in our ancestral law and was zealous for God, just as all of you are today. I persecuted this Way to death, binding both men and women and delivering them to prison. Even the high priest of the whole council of elders can testify on my behalf. For from them I even received letters to the brothers and set out for Damascus to bring back to Jerusalem in chains for punishment those there as well.
>
> Acts 22:1-5

Paul's Memory of Who He Was

I myself once thought that I had to do many things against the name of Jesus the Nazorean, and I did so in Jerusalem. I imprisoned many of the holy ones with the authorization I received from the chief priests, and when they were to put to death I cast my vote against them. Many times, in synagogue after synagogue, I punished them in an attempt to force them to blaspheme; I was so enraged against them that I pursued them even to foreign cities.

Acts 26:8-11

TMIY

Paul Enters the Road to Damascus

Now Saul, still breathing murderous threats against the disciples of the Lord, went to the high priest and asked him for letters to the synagogues in Damascus, that, if he should find any men or women who belonged to the Way, he might bring them back to Jerusalem in chains.

Acts 9:1-2

TMIY

Transformation of Paul's Mind

Therefore, that I might not become too elated, a thorn in the flesh was given to me, an angel of Satan, to beat me, to keep me from being too elated. Three times I begged the Lord about this, that it might leave me, but he said to me, 'My grace is sufficient for you, for power is made perfect in weakness.' I will rather boast most gladly of my weaknesses, in order that the power of Christ may dwell with me. Therefore, I am content with weaknesses, insults, hardships, persecutions, and constraints, for the sake of Christ; for when I am weak, then I am strong.

2 Cor 12:7-10

TMIY

Transformation of Paul's Heart

" I give thanks to my God at every remembrance of you, praying always with joy in my every prayer for all of you, because of your partnership for the gospel from the first day until now... It is right that I should think this way about all of you, because I hold you in my heart, you who are all partners with me in grace... For God is my witness, how I long for all of you with the affection of Christ Jesus. And this is my prayer: that your love may increase ever more.

Phil 1:3-5, 7-9

TMIY

Transformation of Paul's Tongue

" I handed on to you as of first importance what I also received: that Christ died for our sins in accordance with the scriptures; that he was buried; that he was raised on the third day in accordance with the scriptures; that he appeared to Cephas, then to the Twelve. After that, he appeared to more than five hundred brothers at once, most of whom are still living, though some have fallen asleep. After that he appeared to James, then to all the apostles. Last of all, as to one born abnormally, he appeared me.

1 Cor 15:3-8

TMIY

 **Session 10**

THAT MAN IS YOU

- **Does this greater attention to Paul's conversion make Paul more or less relatable to you? Why?**

- **In considering the transformation of the way St. Paul learned to see, learned to listen, and learned to speak, what would you consider the most demanding kind of transformation for you and why?**

Session 11

On Earth As It Is In Heaven

The Last Judgment

> There are only two kinds of people in the end:
> those who say to God, 'Thy will be done,'
> and those to whom God says, 'Thy will be done'.
>
> C. S. Lewis,
> The Great Divorce

TMIY

A Daily Prayer

> My Lord and My God, I beg for the grace that all of my intentions, actions, and operations may be directly purely to the praise and service of Your divine majesty.
>
> St. Ignatius of Loyola,
> Spiritual Exercises 46

TMIY

The Call of the King

It is my will to conquer the whole world and all my enemies, and thus to enter into the glory of my Father. Therefore, whoever wishes to join me in this enterprise must be willing to labor with me, that by following me in suffering, he may follow me in glory.

St. Ignatius of Loyola,
Spiritual Exercises 95

TMIY

The Response to the King

Eternal Lord of all things, in the presence of Thy infinite goodness, and of Thy glorious Mother, and of all the saints of Thy heavenly court, this is the offering of myself which I make with Thy favor and help. I proclaim that it is my earnest desire and my deliberate choice, provided only it is for Thy greater service and praise, to imitate Thee in bearing all wrongs and all abuse and all poverty, both actual and spiritual, should Thy most holy majesty deign to choose and admit me to such a state and way of life.

Spiritual Exercises 98

TMIY

Blessed Franz's Last Letter

Now my dear children, when your mother reads you this letter, your father will already be dead... Out of my experience I can say that life is painful when one lives as a lukewarm Christian. To exist this way is to have more the existence of a vegetable than to truly live. If a person were to possess all of the world's wisdom and be able to claim half the earth as his own, he could and would still be less fortunate than a poor person who can claim nothing in this world as his own other than a deep Catholic faith...

TMIY

Blessed Franz's Last Letter

> I would not exchange my small, dirty cell for a king's palace if I was required to give up even a small part of my faith.
>
> All that is earthly—no matter how much, nor how beautiful—comes to an end. But God's Word is eternal.
>
> Blessed Franz Jägerstätter
> Letters and Writings from Prison

TMIY

Session 11

THAT MAN IS YOU!

- **How does St. Ignatius's emphasis on serving the Lord as if responding to the Call of a King strengthen, challenge, or change your life as a disciple?**

- **Following Blessed Franz Jägerstätter, what does it mean for you to put God first as a husband, or father, or man of God?**

My Son, Jonathan

A Wounded Man

> In our own woundedness, we can become a source of life for others.
>
> - Fr. Henri Nouwen, Wounded Healer

TMIY

Blinded

> Father, forgive them;
> for they know not what they do.
>
> –Luke 23:34

TMIY

A Life of Dissipation

Not many days later, the younger son gathered all he had and took his journey into a far country, and there he squandered his property in loose living.

–Luke 15:13

TMIY

The Haunting of the Past

I have long since feared that the sins of my past would come back to haunt me, and the cost is more than I could bear.

– The Patriot

TMIY

Steps of the Healing Process

1 General Confession	4
2	5
3	6

TMIY

Hope, Patience, Persistence

> "
> Rejoice in your hope, be patient in tribulation,
> be constant in prayer.
>
> —Romans 12:12 "

Continuous Pain

> "
> Why is my pain unceasing, my wound incurable,
> refusing to be healed?
>
> —Jeremiah 15:18 "

Steps of the Healing Process

1	General Confession	4	
2	Discuss Issue w/ Spouse	5	
3		6	

Steps of the Healing Process

1	General Confession	**4**	
2	Discuss Issue w/ Spouse	**5**	
3	Name My Son	**6**	

TMIY

Steps of the Healing Process

1	General Confession	**4**	Call Former Girlfriend
2	Discuss Issue w/ Spouse	**5**	
3	Name My Son	**6**	

TMIY

Strength In Christ

> " I can do all things in him who strengthens me.
>
> – Philippians 4:13 "

TMIY

Steps of the Healing Process

1	General Confession	4	Call Former Girlfriend
2	Discuss Issue w/ Spouse	5	Show Wounds to Others
3	Name My Son	6	

Steps of the Healing Process

1	General Confession	4	Call Former Girlfriend
2	Discuss Issue w/ Spouse	5	Show Wounds to Others
3	Name My Son	6	Letter to My Son

The Foolishness of God

> "
> For the foolishness of God is wiser than men, and the weakness of God is stronger than men.
>
> –1 Corinthians 1:25 "

•Have you ever made a decision in your life that you know was wrong and sinful in nature and instead of bringing it to Confession, you felt that your best "path forward" was burying it deep inside your heart in an attempt to avoid the pain? Were you successful in your attempt to alleviate the pain? If not, what can you do now to lift the burden?

•Have you ever brought a mortal sin to confession and received God's unconditional forgiveness, only to turn around and not forgive yourself for the transgression? How do you think God views your lack of personal forgiveness?

Session 13

The Kingdom is Like Weeds Among the Wheat

The Parable of Weeds Among the Wheat

> The kingdom of heaven may be compared to a man who sowed good seed in his field; but while men were sleeping, his enemy came and sowed weeds among the wheat, and went away. So when the plants came up and bore grain, then the weeds appeared also.
>
> -Matthew 13:24-26

TMIY

The Enemy

> 'How then has it weeds?' He said to them, 'An enemy has done this.'
>
> -Matthew 13:27-28

TMIY

Virtue

Vir = Man

Viribus = Strength

Virtue = a habitual and firm disposition to do the good.

Discernment

Allows you to see the good from the bad.

To Be Human

Humus = earth or ground; dirt

To be human is to be humble.

> The Lord God formed man of dust from the ground, and breathed into his nostrils the breath of life; and man became a living being.
>
> -Genesis 2:7

TMIY

Succulent Fried Chicken Breast over a Wedge Salad w/ Greens

TMIY

Succulent Fried Chicken Breast over a Wedge Salad w/ Greens

Ingredients:

Chicken
- 1 Chicken Breast
- ½ cup Mayonnaise
- 2 Tbs water
- 1 box Panko Breadcrumbs
- 1 box Italian seasoned breadcrumbs
- ½ tsp Cayenne pepper
- 4Tbs/Half stick of butter
- 4Tbs Olive oil
- ½ -1 tsp Salt
- ½ - 1 tsp Pepper

Salad Dressing
- ¼ cup sour cream
- ¼ cup mayonnaise
- ½ tsp salt
- ½ tsp garlic powder
- Dash of Tabasco sauce
- Dash of Worcestershire sauce
- ½ Tbs water
- Dash of Ground black pepper
- 1 bunch chives thinly sliced (apx 1 Tbs)

Salad
- 1 Head iceberg lettuce, cut into a wedge
- 1 bag arugula, 1 large "pinch" apx ⅛ cup
- 1 container pea sprouts or microgreens, 1 large "pinch" apx ⅛ cup
- 1 container mint leaves, 6-8 leaves, ripped
- Crispy bacon bit, apx 2 Tbs
- Dried cranberries, apx 1 Tbs
- Cherry tomatoes halved, apx 3-4 tomatoes per person

Instructions:

Chicken
- Filet chicken breast in half and season on both sides with salt and pepper.
- In a medium sized bowl combine mayonnaise, water, and cayenne pepper and mix until smooth.
- In a separate bowl/container add equal parts panko breadcrumbs and Italian seasoned breadcrumbs and mix.
- Dredge the chicken in the wet ingredients followed by the breadcrumb mix and repeat a second time. Making sure the chicken has an even coating of breadcrumbs on the outside.
- Add ½ a stick of butter and 4 tbs of olive oil to a pan and heat to 350 degrees Fahrenheit.
- Once the oil is up to temp, add the breaded chicken breasts to the pan and cook, flipping halfway, until 165 degrees internally and a nice golden-brown exterior (roughly 10 minutes).
- Once done, place the chicken onto a wire rack or paper towel lined plate to rest before cutting into strips.

Salad
- In a large bowl combine sour cream, mayonnaise, salt, garlic powder, Tabasco sauce, Worcestershire sauce, ground black pepper, chives, and ½ tsp water (add more or less to get the desired consistency) and whisk until combined.
- Combine a handful of arugula, some mint leaves, pea sprouts or microgreens, bacon bits, and dried cranberries in a bowl and dress with a desired amount of house-made salad dressing.

Plating
- Slice a ½ inch thick slice of the iceberg lettuce head and place it on the plate as the foundation of the dish and season it lightly with salt and pepper.
- Take a handful of dressed salad mix and place it on top of the iceberg wedge slice and top with halved cherry tomatoes.
- Slice chicken on a bias and place on top of the salad, and garnish with extra chives and microgreens.

Session 13

- What are the weeds in your life that can, by God's grace, be turned into virtue?

- How are you growing in the virtue of humility?

Session 14

Resilience and Perseverance

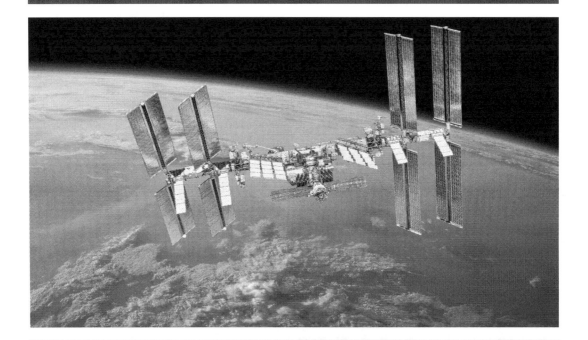

Setting Your Target

> The only real sadness, the only real failure, the only great tragedy in life, is not to become a saint.
>
> -Léon Bloy

Resilience and Perseverance

<u>Resilience</u>:
The capacity to recover quickly from difficulties; toughness.
<u>Perseverance</u>:
Continued effort to do or achieve something despite difficulties, failure, or opposition.

Obstacles and Setbacks

<u>The 7 Deadly Sins</u>:
Pride, Lust, Greed, Gluttony, Sloth, Wrath, Envy
<u>Fruits of the Spirit</u>:
Love, joy, peace, patience, kindness, goodness, faithfulness, gentleness, and self control

Hitting Your Target: A Daily Plan

1	A Gesture of Love, Surrender, Trust	6	Angelus at Noon
2	Morning Prayer	7	Divine Mercy at 3pm
3	Rosary	8	Prayer Before Meals
4	Silence	9	Evening Prayer with Family
5	Mass	10	Throughout the Day: Come Holy Spirit

Hitting Your Target: A Weekly Plan

1 Mass On Sunday

2 Joy With Family

3 Set Mind on Things Above

4 Spiritual Conversations

5 Active Evangelization

TMIY

Hitting Your Target: A Monthly Plan

Confession

TMIY

Hitting Your Target: A Yearly Plan

1 A Retreat or Pilgrimage

2 A Day of Silence

3 A Strong Lenten Journey

TMIY

The Exhilaration of Discoveries

 We are in a tough business. It is like climbing Mt. Everest. No matter how good you are, you are going to lose your grip sometimes and fall back. Then you have a choice, either retreat to the relative comfort and safety of the base camp, or get up, dust yourself off, get a firmer grip and a surer toehold and head back up for the summit. The space business is not about base camps. It is about summits. And, the exhilaration of discoveries you make once you get there. That is what drives you on. -Dr. Firouz Naderi, NASA

TMIY

TMIY | **Session 14**
THAT MAN IS YOU!

• Do you have a clearly defined Mission Statement for your life? How about for your family? Do your family members know their primary mission - to get to Heaven?

• With the help of your small group and lots of prayer, begin building the plan for your spiritual life: Daily, Weekly, Monthly, Yearly.

Session 15

Son of Man, Do You See?

Spiritual Gifts From God

And his gifts were that some should be apostles, some prophets, some evangelists, some pastors and teachers, to equip the saints for the work of ministry for building up the body of Christ, until we all attain to the unity of the faith and of the knowledge of the Son of God, to mature manhood, to the measure of the stature of the fulness of Christ, so that we may no longer be children tossed back and forth and carried about with every wind of doctrine, by the cunning of men, by their craftiness in deceitful wiles.

- Ephesians 4:11-14

TMIY

Earnestly Desire the Spiritual Gifts

Make love your aim, and earnestly desire the spiritual gifts, especially that you may prophesy.

- 1 Corinthians 14:1

TMIY

Hold Fast to What is Good

Do not quench the Spirit, do not despise prophesying, but test everything, hold fast what is good, abstain from every form of evil.

- 1 Thessalonians 5:19-22

TMIY

The Economic System

Son of man, do you see that city going bankrupt? Are you willing to see all your cities going bankrupt? Are you willing to see the bankruptcy of the whole economic system you rely on now so that all money is worthless and cannot support you?

- Fr. Michael Scanlan Prophesy, 1976

TMIY

Crime and Lawlessness

Son of man, do you see the crime and lawlessness in your city streets, and towns, and institutions? Are you willing to see no law, no order, no protection for you except that which I myself will give you?

- Fr. Michael Scanlan Prophesy, 1976

TMIY

The Country You Love

Son of man, do you see the country which you love and which you are now celebrating—a country's history that you look back on with nostalgia? Are you willing to see no country—no country to call your own except those I give you as my body? Will you let me bring you life in my body and only there?

- Fr. Michael Scanlan Prophesy, 1976

TMIY

Churches Shut Down

Son of man, do you see those churches which you can go to so easily now? Are you ready to see them with bars across their doors, with doors nailed shut? Are you ready to base your life only on me and not on any particular structure? Are you ready to depend only on me and not on all the institutions of schools and parishes that you are working so hard to foster?

- Fr. Michael Scanlan Prophesy, 1976

TMIY

The Structures are Falling

Son of man, I call you to be ready for that. That is what I am telling you about. The structures are falling and changing—it is not for you to know the details now—but do not rely on them as you have been. I want you to make a deeper commitment to one another. I want you to trust one another, to build an interdependence that is based on my Spirit. It is an interdependence that is no luxury.

- Fr. Michael Scanlan Prophesy, 1976

TMIY

This is My Word

> It is an absolute necessity for those who will base their lives on me and not the structures from a pagan world. I have spoken and it will take place. My word will go forth to my people. They may hear and they may not—and I will respond accordingly—but this is my word.
>
> - Fr. Michael Scanlan Prophesy, 1976

A Sign Has Been Given

> Look about you, son of man. When you see it all shut down, when you see everything removed which has been taken for granted, and when you are prepared to live without these things, then you will know what I am making ready.
>
> - Fr. Michael Scanlan Prophesy, 1976

TMIY — Session 15

- What most struck you about Fr. Michael Scanlan's prophecy?

- What practical implications do you think it may have for your life and for the life of your family?

Session 16

The Time for Purification

A Time for Purification

The Lord God says, "Hear My Word: The time that has been marked by My blessings and gifts is being replaced now by the period to be marked by my judgment and purification. What I have not accomplished by blessings and gifts, I will accomplish by judgment and purification."

- Fr. Michael Scanlan Prophesy, 1980

TMIY

Fragmentation and Confusion

There is fragmentation, confusion, throughout the ranks. Satan goes where he will and infects whom he will. He has free access throughout my people —and I will not stand for this.

- Fr. Michael Scanlan Prophesy, 1980

TMIY

Fear of the World or Fear of the Lord

They are more determined by fear of what others will think of them—fears of failure and rejection in the world, loss of respect of neighbors and superiors and those around them—than they are determined by fear of me and fear of infidelity to my word ... You cannot be considered at this point in the center of the battle and the conflict that is going on.

- Fr. Michael Scanlan Prophesy, 1980

TMIY

A Difficult and Necessary Time

So this time is now come upon all of you: a time of judgment and of purification. Sin will be called sin. Satan will be unmasked. Fidelity will be held up for what it is and should be. My faithful servants will be seen and will come together. They will not be many in number. It will be a difficult and a necessary time. There will be collapse, difficulties throughout the world.

- Fr. Michael Scanlan Prophesy, 1980

TMIY

To Whom Shall We Go

There will be purification and persecution among my people. You will have to stand for what you believe. You will have to choose between the world and me. You will have to choose what word you will follow and whom you will respect.

- Fr. Michael Scanlan Prophesy, 1980

TMIY

Refiner's Fire

> And in that choice, what has not been accomplished by the time of blessing and gifts will be accomplished. What has not been accomplished in the baptism and the flooding of gifts of my Spirit will be accomplished in a baptism of fire. The fire will move among you and it will burn out what is chaff. The fire will move among you individually, corporately, in groups, and around the world.
>
> — Fr. Michael Scanlan Prophesy, 1980

TMIY

Total Submission

> What you need to do is to come before Me in total submission to My Word, in total submission to My plan, in the total submission in this new hour. What you need to do is to drop the things that are your own, those things of the past. What you need to do is to see yourselves and those whom you have responsibility for in light of this hour of judgment and purification. You need to see them in that way and do for them what will best help them to stand strong and be among My faithful servants.
>
> — Fr. Michael Scanlan Prophesy, 1980

TMIY

My People, My Church, My Spirit

> For there will be casualties. It will not be easy, but it is necessary. It is necessary that My people be, in fact, my people; that My Church be, in fact, My Church; and that My Spirit, in fact, bring forth the purity of life, the purity and fidelity to the Gospel.
>
> — Fr. Michael Scanlan Prophesy, 1980

TMIY

Session 16

•What most struck you about Fr. Michael Scanlan's prophecy?

•What practical implications do you think it may have for your life and for the life of your family?

Session 17

The Kingdom is Like A Dragnet

Ichthus in Greek

The Ichthus ("Fish"): An Acronym

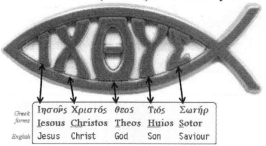

Greek forms	Ἰησοῦς	Χριστός	θεος	Υἱός	Σωτήρ
	Iesous	Christos	Theos	Huios	Sotor
English	Jesus	Christ	God	Son	Saviour

The Parable of The Dragnet

 Again, the kingdom of heaven is like a net which was thrown into the sea and gathered fish of every kind; when it was full, men drew it ashore and sat down and sorted the good into vessels but threw away the bad. So it will be at the close of the age. The angels will come out and separate the evil from the righteous, and throw them into the furnace of fire; there men will weep and gnash their teeth.
-Matthew 13:47-50

Peace with Rest on You

> Whatever house you enter, first say, 'Peace be to this house!' And if a son of peace is there, your peace shall rest upon him; but if not, it shall return to you.
>
> -Luke 10:5-6

TMIY

Evangelization Tool

> Whenever you enter a town and they receive you, eat what is set before you.
>
> -Luke 10:8

TMIY

Discernment

Being able to measure out the good from the bad.

TMIY

Jesus Knows How to Catch Fish

> Put out into the deep and
> let down your nets for a catch.
>
> -Luke 5:4

TMIY

Be Good Bait

Be an attractive example of the
faith.

TMIY

Humility and the Kingdom

> Blessed are the poor in spirit, for theirs
> is the kingdom of heaven.
>
> -Matthew 5:3

TMIY

17-3

Those Who Are Hungry

> Blessed are those who hunger and thirst for righteousness, for they shall be satisfied.
>
> -Matthew 5:6

Seared Tuna Steak w/ Umami Broccoli and Gremolata Sauce

Seared Tuna Steak w/ Umami Broccoli and Gremolata Sauce

Ingredients:

Fish
- 1 tuna steak
- ½-1 tsp Salt
- ½-1 tsp Ground black pepper
- 1-2 Tbs olive oil
- 1 Tbs butter

Broccoli
- 1 head broccoli
- 1 Tbs butter
- 3 cloves minced garlic
- 2 Tbs olive oil
- 4 anchovy filets
- 1/4 tsp red chili pepper
- Dash of salt
- 1/2 cup white wine
- Parmesan (optional)

Warm & Creamy Gremolata
- Zest of 1 lemon
- 4 thin slices of lemon, minced
- 2-3 chives minced
- 1/3 bunch parsley minced
- 5 cloves garlic minced
- ½ cup white wine
- ½ cup heavy cream
- 1 Tbs capers with brine
- Dash of tabasco
- Dash of salt
- Dash of ground black pepper

Instructions:

Broccoli
- Cut broccoli into florets.
- Add butter, olive oil, minced garlic, and anchovy filets into a medium-high heat pan and cook until the anchovy filets melts away or breaks down into the sauce.
- Add the broccoli florets and chili pepper into the pan, stir occasionally.
- Finish broccoli with a dash of salt and deglaze the pan with ½ cup of white wine.
- Cook until the wine is reduced, and the broccoli is fork tender but still slightly crunchy (about 7 to 8 minutes).

Tuna with the Warm & Creamy Gremolata
- In a small bowl combine the zest of a lemon, 4 small lemon slices, chives, parsley, and minced garlic, and set aside.
- Season the tuna steak lightly with salt and pepper on both sides.
- Heat up olive oil in a high heat pan and add the tuna, the pan needs to be hot for the tuna to get a nice sear on the outside.
- After 1.5 minutes flip the tuna, add 1 Tbs of butter into the pan, let it melt and use a spoon to baste over the top of the tuna for another 1.5 minutes. Note: The tuna will only cook for about 3 minutes total, the outside will have a sear, but the inside should still be nice and pink.
- Using a spatula put the finished tuna onto a plate to rest and set it aside. Take the pan that you used to cook the tuna and place it back on the heat to make the gremolata.
- Once the pan is hot again, add the gremolata mix that we had set aside before to the pan, then deglaze with ½ cup of white wine.
- Once all the alcohol is cooked out of the wine and it is slightly reduced add ½ cup of heavy cream, 1 Tbs capers with brine, a dash of tabasco sauce, as well as a dash of salt and pepper and your sauce is done.

Plating
This dish can be plated simply, take a spoonful of the gremolata sauce and put it down on the plate. Place the fish on top of it with the broccoli around the sides and top the fish with a garnish of parsley and lemon.

- How are you good bait? Are you attracting people into the love of God? What are you doing to bring people into your home?

- How do you create texture for your family? Do you simply make faith so hard without sweetness?

Session 18

Just a Guy in the Pew

Joy in Heaven

> There will be more joy in heaven over one sinner
> who repents than over ninety-nine righteous
> persons who need no repentance.
>
> -Luke 15:7

TMIY

A Message for Young People

> Freedom is a good thing if you know who
> you are.
>
> -John Edwards

TMIY

Wearing Masks

> From the outside looking in I had everything. I had money. I had a great job. It looked like I was a wonderful person... but inside I was a broken-down mess... I was hiding everything. I wore mask after mask.
>
> -John Edwards

TMIY

A Firm Hand

> Son, that is not up to you. That is up to God. If you want forgiveness, then you need to be serious about your forgiveness and not give God terms.
>
> -Priest in Confession

TMIY

Moment of Clarity

> And in this moment where there should be nothing but stress, worry and anxiety, this tremendous peace came over me. And all of a sudden I heard myself say the truest words I have ever said in my life: Well at least now I don't have to lie anymore. At least everyone will know who I am.
>
> -John Edwards

TMIY

The Power of Vulnerability

 That is the night that God showed me the power of vulnerability in our lives. You know as men, we are told to just be quiet, don't complain, put your head down, work hard, don't have emotions, nobody cares, everybody's got there own problems. The world tells you that to be vulnerable is to be susceptible to attack, weak, unmasculine... [but the] Lord says no, my power is made perfect in weakness. -John Edwards

TMIY

Boasting in Our Weakness

 So, I will boast all the more gladly of my weaknesses, so that the power of Christ may dwell in me. Therefore I am content with weaknesses, insults, hardships, persecutions, and calamities for the sake of Christ; for whenever I am weak, then I am strong.

-2 Corinthians 12:9-10

TMIY

TMIY **Session 18**
THAT MAN IS YOU!

• What masks are you currently wearing in your life?

• Have you become vulnerable with the Lord?

• Do you believe that God has forgiven you for your mistakes and that you are his beloved son?

Session 19

The Narrow Gate

The Kingdom of God

> For the kingdom of God does not mean food and drink but righteousness and peace and joy in the Holy Spirit.
>
> - Romans 14:17

TMIY

Thy Kingdom Come

> The kingdom of God [is] righteousness and peace and joy in the Holy Spirit. The end-time in which we live is the age of the outpouring of the Spirit. Ever since Pentecost, a decisive battle has been joined between "the flesh" and the Spirit.
>
> Only a pure soul can boldly say: "Thy kingdom come." One who has heard Paul say, "Let not sin therefore reign in your mortal bodies," and has purified himself in action, thought and word will say to God: "Thy kingdom come!"
>
> CCC 2819

TMIY

The Beatitudes

Blessed are the poor in spirit, for theirs is the kingdom of heaven.
Blessed are those who mourn, for they shall be comforted.
Blessed are the meek, for they shall inherit the earth.
Blessed are those who hunger and thirst for righteousness, for they shall be satisfied.
Blessed are the merciful, for they shall obtain mercy.
Blessed are the pure in heart, for they shall see God.
Blessed are the peacemakers, for they shall be called sons of God.
Blessed are those who are persecuted for righteousness' sake, for theirs is the kingdom of heaven.   - Matthew 5: 3-10

Entering the Kingdom

For I tell you, unless your righteousness exceeds that of the scribes and Pharisees, you will never enter the kingdom of heaven.

- Matthew 5:20

The Narrow Gate

Enter by the narrow gate; for the gate is wide and the way is easy, that leads to destruction, and those who enter by it are many. For the gate is narrow and the way is hard, that leads to life, and those who find it are few.

- Matthew 7:13-14

Hearers and Doers

"Every one then who hears these words of mine and does them will be like a wise man who built his house upon the rock; and the rain fell, and the floods came, and the winds blew and beat upon that house, but it did not fall, because it had been founded on the rock. And every one who hears these words of mine and does not do them will be like a foolish man who built his house upon the sand; and the rain fell, and the floods came, and the winds blew and beat against that house, and it fell; and great was the fall of it." And when Jesus finished these sayings, the crowds were astonished at his teaching.

- Matthew 7: 24-28

TMIY

Self-Deception

Not every one who says to me, 'Lord, Lord,' shall enter the kingdom of heaven, but he who does the will of my Father who is in heaven. On that day many will say to me, 'Lord, Lord, did we not prophesy in your name, and cast out demons in your name, and do many mighty works in your name?' And then will I declare to them, 'I never knew you; depart from me, you evildoers.'

- Matthew 7: 21-23

TMIY

The Multitude or The Few

If you wish to imitate the multitude, then you shall not be among the few who enter through the narrow gate.

- St. Augustine

TMIY

The Minority

> " Those who are saved are in the minority.
>
> — St. Thomas Aquinas "

As You Live

> " As a man lives so shall he die.
>
> — St. Augustine "

Perseverance

> " Many begin well, but there are few who persevere.
>
> — St. Jerome "

A State of Lukewarmness

St Teresa, as the Roman Rota attests, never fell into any mortal sin but still our Lord showed her the place prepared for her in Hell: not because she deserved hell, but because, had she not risen from the state of lukewarmness, she would in the end have lost the grace of God and been damned.

- St. Alphonsos

TMIY

TMIY Session 19
THAT MAN IS YOU!

- When is the last time you have hungered for God, for righteousness?
- Does the way I live my faith look more like a hobby or a way of life?
- Where is your treasure? Wherever it is is where your heart will be.
- Have I truly repented of my former way of life and given my life to the Lord?
- Do I know Jesus Christ and am I living in His ways?

Session 20

A Tale of Two Cities

The First Preaching of Christ

The time is fulfilled, and the kingdom of God is at hand; repent, and believe in the gospel.

Mark 1:15

TMIY

A Reluctant King

When the people saw the sign which he had done, they said, 'This is indeed the prophet who is to come into the world!' Perceiving then that they were about to come and take him by force to make him king, Jesus withdrew again to the hills by himself.

John 6:14-15

TMIY

A Puzzling Victory

> They gave a sum of money to the soldiers and said, 'Tell people, `His disciples came by night and stole him away while we were asleep`. And if this comes to the governor's ears, we will satisfy him and keep you out of trouble. So they took the money and did as they were directed; and this story has been spread among Jews to this day.

Matthew 28:12-15

TMIY

The Church would struggle for centuries to understand the "kingdom of God."

St. Augustine gave the "classic" answer in his masterpiece, The City of God.

The context is important.

TMIY

The Fall of Rome

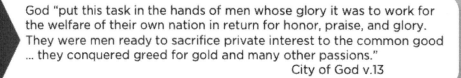

God "put this task in the hands of men whose glory it was to work for the welfare of their own nation in return for honor, praise, and glory. They were men ready to sacrifice private interest to the common good ... they conquered greed for gold and many other passions."
City of God v.13

"In place of these virtues, we have ... public need and private opulence ... we rob virtue to reward ambition. No wonder – with each one consulting his own interest, thinking only of lust at home and of fortune or favors in public life – that the republic is helpless to defend itself."
City of God v.12

Source: Augustine, "City of God," The Fathers of the Church, v. 8, The Catholic University of America Press, Washington, DC, 1950, p. 273 and p. 271.

TMIY

The Critical Issue: Love

 There are, then, two loves, of which one is holy, the other unclean; one turned towards the neighbor, the other centered on self; one looking to the common good, keeping in view the society of saints in heaven, the other bringing the common good under its own power, arrogantly looking to domination ... one wishing for its neighbor what it wishes for itself, the other seeking to subject its neighbor to itself.

-The Literal Meaning of Genesis XI.15

Source: Augustine, The Literal Meaning of Genesis, v.2, Ancient Christian Writers, No. 42, Newman Press, New York, 1958, p. 128.

TMIY

Two Loves ... Two Cities

 Two cities, then, have been created by two loves: that is, the earthly by love of self extending even to contempt of God, and the heavenly by love of God extending to contempt of self.

-City of God, XIV.28

Source: Augustine, "City of God," Trans. Dyson, R.W., Cambridge University Press, Cambridge, UK, 1998, p. 632.

TMIY

A Heavenly Mystery

 These two loves started among the angels, one love in the good angels, the other in the bad; and they have marked the limits of the two cities established among men.

-The Literal Meaning of Genesis, XI.15

Source: Augustine, The Literal Meaning of Genesis, v.2, Ancient Christian Writers, No. 42, Newman Press, New York, 1958, p. 128.

TMIY

An Enduring Mystery

Can we anywise now separate them from each other? They are mingled, and from the very beginning of mankind mingled they run on unto the end of the world ... but at the end to be severed.

-Commentary Psalm 65, 2

Source: Augustine, Expositions on the Book of Psalms, Nicene and Post-Nicene Fathers, First Series, v. 8, Ed. Schaff, P., Hendrickson Publishers, Peabody, MA, 1994, p. 268.

TMIY

 This is not abstract theology only relevant to Rome!

It relates to us today.

The two cities remain in conflict.

TMIY

The Confrontation of Modern Times

 The world is facing "the greatest historical confrontation humanity has gone through ... the final confrontation between the Church and the anti-Church, or the Gospel and the anti-Gospel."
Karol Cardinal Wojtyla
International Eucharistic Conference

 "In our times evil had grown disproportionately, operating through perverted systems which have practiced violence and elimination on a vast scale. The evil of the twentieth century was not a small-scale evil, it was not simply 'homemade.' It was an evil of gigantic proportions."
Pope St. John Paul II, Memory and Identity

Source: Wojtyla, K., quoted in Wall Street Journal, November 9, 1978.
Pope John Paul II, "Memory and Identity," Rizzoli, 2005, p. 167.

TMIY

The 'Vision' of Pope St. John Paul II

> Ricoeur has called Freud, Marx and Nietzsche 'masters of suspicion', having in mind the whole system each one represents, and perhaps above all the hidden basis and orientation of each in understanding and interpreting the humanum itself ... the thinkers mentioned above, who have exercised and still exercise a great influence on the way of thinking and evaluating people of our time, seem in substance also to judge and accuse the human heart.
>
> -St. John Paul II

Source: Pope St. John Paul II, Wednesday Audience, October 29, 1980.

TMIY

The Enslavement of the Heart

Friedrich Nietzsche

Master of Suspicion

Karl Marx

Sigmund Freud

Nietzsche	The Pride of Life
Marx	The Concupiscence of the Eyes
Freud	The Concupiscence of the Flesh

Source: Pope St. John Paul II, Wednesday Audience, October 29, 1980.

TMIY

Friedrich Nietzsche

"God is dead ... we have killed him."

"Man is something that shall be overcome... All beings so far have created something beyond themselves... You have made your way from work to man, and much in you is still worm ... Behold, I teach you the overman."

"O my brothers, am I cruel? I say: what is falling, we should still push... I am a prelude of better players, O my brothers! Follow my precedent. And he whom you cannot teach to fly, teach to fall fasters.

"I know my fate. One day there will be associated with my name the recollection of something frightful... of a crisis like no other before on earth. There will be wars such as there have never yet been on earth."

Source: "The Portable Nietzsche," Trans. Kaufmann, W., Penguin Books, 1954-1982, p. 95, p. 124, p. 321. Nietzsche, F., "Ecce Homo," Trans. Hollingdale, R., Penguin Classics, 2004, pp. 96-97.

TMIY

War: To Be Overpowered

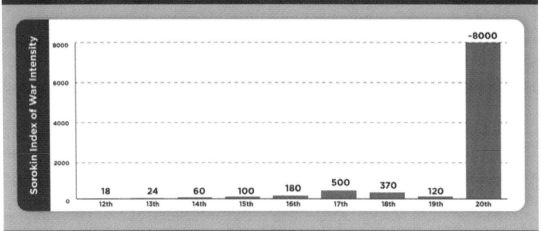

Source: Sorokin, P., "Social and Cultural Dynamics," v. 4, Table 49, p. 655. Author estimate for 20th Century extrapolated based upon Sorokin value after WWI.

TMIY

Karl Marx

> "Individuals are dealt with only in so far as they are personifications of economic categories, embodiments of particular class-relations and class-interests."

> "The method of production in material life determines the general character of the social, political, and spiritual processes of life. It is not the consciousness of men that determines their being, but on the contrary, their social being determines their consciousness."

> "Then I will wander godlike and victorious through the world and giving my words and active force, I will feel equal to the Creator."

Source: "Das Kapital," in The Portable Marx, ed. Kamenka, E., Penguin Books, New York, 1983, p. 435.
"The German Ideology," quoted in "Darwin, Marx, Wagner – Critique of a Heritage," Barzun, J., The University of Chicago Press, 1941-1981, p. 133.
McLellan, D., "Karl Marx: His Life and Thought," Harper Row, New York, 1974, p. 22.

TMIY

Famine: Economic Collapse

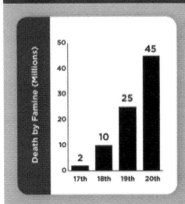

1917: "Peace, land, bread" – Vladimir Lenin.

1917: Communist Revolution followed by Civil War - 9 million deaths.

1921: 1 to 3 million die in Russian Famine.

1932-1934: 5 to 10 million die in Russian Famine.

1958-1961: 20-30 million die in Chinese Famine.

During the 1970's in Russia, food production increased 1% per year, one half of all farms operated at a loss, one-fifth to one-third of crops rotted in ground for lack of adequate storage, and food imports increased 1000%.

Source: Arnold, D., "Famine – Social Crisis and Historical Change," Basil Blackwell, 1991, p. 20.
Carroll, W., "The Rise and Fall of the Communist Revolution," Christendom Press, 1935, p. 695.

TMIY

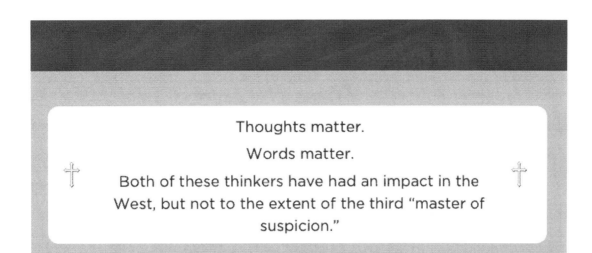

Thoughts matter.

Words matter.

Both of these thinkers have had an impact in the West, but not to the extent of the third "master of suspicion."

TMIY

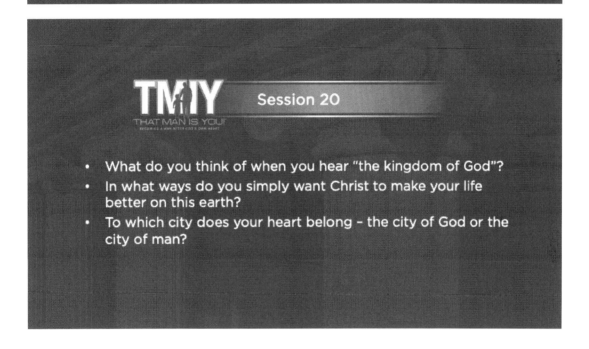

Session 20

- What do you think of when you hear "the kingdom of God"?
- In what ways do you simply want Christ to make your life better on this earth?
- To which city does your heart belong – the city of God or the city of man?

Session 21

The Darkness of Modern Culture

✝ Last time we considered the City of God and the City of Man.

We considered two ideologies of evil.

This week it hits close to home. ✝

TMIY

The Enslavement of the Heart

Nietzsche	The Pride of Life
Marx	The Concupiscence of the Eyes
Freud	The Concupiscence of the Flesh

Source: Pope St. John Paul II, Wednesday Audience, October 29, 1980.

TMIY

Technology as Transformation

> Millions today embrace the Pill as a salvation ... Many attribute to the Pill more than to anything else the sexual revolution of the 1960s ... As it was intended to do, the Pill has disconnected fear of pregnancy from the pursuit of sexual pleasure ... The Pill has led each of us ... into a new era of potential mastery over our bodies and ourselves ... We have passed through the gateway ... We have entered the Age of Bio Intervention.

Source: Asbell, B., "The Pill: A Biography of the Drug that Changed the World," Random House, New York, 1995, p. 7 and p. 366.

TMIY

The Transformation of Marriage

Divorce

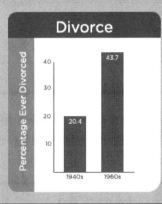

Research

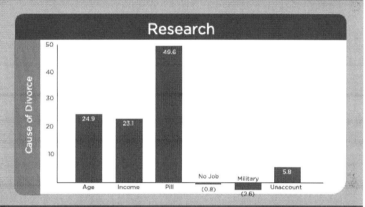

Source: General Social Survey, 1972-2020
Michael, R., "Why Did the U.S. Divorce Rate Double Within A Decade?" Research in Population Economics, 1988.

TMIY

The Transformation of Faith

Church Attendance

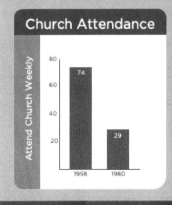

Marital Structure

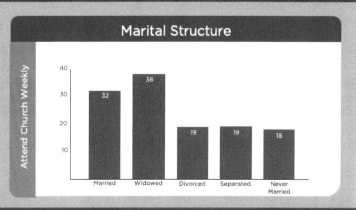

Source: Gallup Poll and General Social Survey, 1972-2018.

TMIY

The first major step down was with the Pill in 1960.

The next major step down was with the technological revolution around 2000.

TMIY

A Technological Perfect Storm

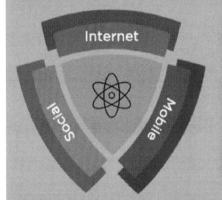

Internet	Developed in 1960s, the internet was commercialized in the 1990s. Microsoft Windows 95/98 brought it to average computer.
Social Media	Facebook was developed at Harvard in 2003. It opened to everyone in 2006. Social media is preferred media for youth.
Mobile	iPhone was introduced in 2008. It was the world's fastest adopted technology. It has allowed everyone to remained plugged in.

TMIY

The Collapse of Marriage/Family Life

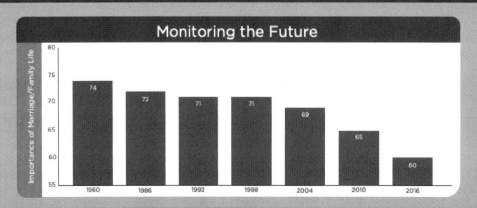

Source: Monitoring the Future, taken from Twenge, J., iGen: Why Today's Super-Connected Kids are Growing Up Less Rebellious, More Tolerant, Less Happy-and Completely Unprepared for Adulthood," Atria Books, New York, 2017, p. 220.

TMIY

The Collapse of Faith

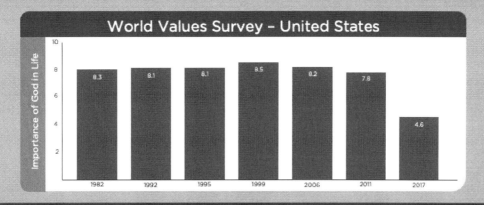

World Values Survey – United States

Importance of God in Life

1982	1992	1995	1999	2006	2011	2017
8.3	8.1	8.1	8.5	8.2	7.8	4.6

Source: World Values Survey, 1982-2017.

TMIY

A Fundamental Reality

 Man cannot live without love ... his life is senseless, if love is not revealed to him, if he does not encounter love, if he does not experience it and make it his own, if he does not participate intimately in it."

-Pope St. John Paul II, Redemptor Hominis, #10

TMIY

Depression Among Girls

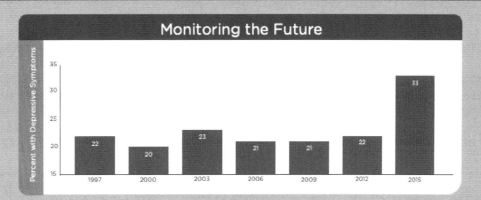

Monitoring the Future

Percent with Depressive Symptoms

1997	2000	2003	2006	2009	2012	2015
22	20	23	21	21	22	33

Source: Monitoring the Future, taken from Twenge, J., iGen: Why Today's Super-Connected Kids are Growing Up Less Rebellious, More Tolerant, Less Happy-and Completely Unprepared for Adulthood," Atria Books, New York, 2017, p. 103.

TMIY

The other two ideologies of evil collapsed according to the very thing they idolized.

Our path may be no different.

TMIY

Fertility Change in the Life of a Couple

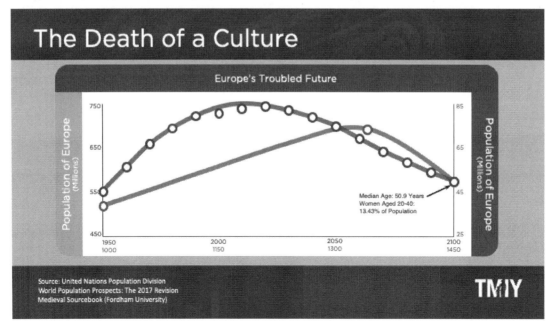

Source: Thoma, M., et al. "Prevalence of infertility in the United States as estimated by the current duration approach and a traditional construct approach," Fertility and Sterility, April 2013.
Slama, R., et al. "Estimation of the frequency of involuntary infertility on a nation-wide basis," Human Reproduction, 2012.
Karmaus, W., et al. "Infertility and subfecundity in population-based samples from Denmark, Germany, Italy, Poland and Spain," European Journal of Public Health, 1999.

Source: Carlsen, E., et al. "Evidence for Decreasing Quality of Semen During Past 50 Years," British Medical Journal, September 12, 1992.
Roland, M., et al. "Decline in semen concentration and morphology in a sample of 26,609 men close to general population between 1989 and 2005 in France," Reproductive Epidemiology, 2012.
Bonde, J., et al. "Relation between semen quality and fertility: a population-based study of 430 first pregnancy planners," The Lancet, October 10, 1998.

Source: The World Bank (1960-2019)
Hamilton, B., et al. "Births: Provisional Data for 2020," CDC, Vital Statistics Rapid Release, Report No. 012, May 2021 (for 2020 data).

TMIY

The Death of a Culture

TMIY

Source: United Nations Population Division
World Population Prospects: The 2017 Revision
Medieval Sourcebook (Fordham University)

However, there is a darker side to this culture.

It is destroying our children.

TMIY

A Darkness for the Next Generation

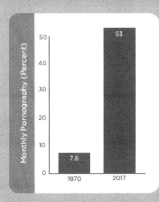

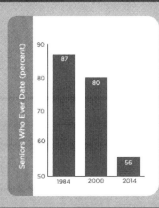

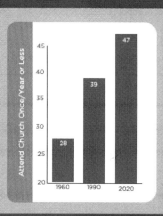

Source: 1970 estimate based on Playboy circulation rate of 5.4 million per month and adult male population of 70.96 million. Regnerus, M., "Relationships in America Survey," reported in "Cheap Sex," Oxford University Press, 2017, p. 117.

Source: Monitoring the Future, taken from Twenge, J., iGen: Why Today's Super-Connected Kids are Growing Up Less Rebellious, More Tolerant, Less Happy-and Completely Unprepared for Adulthood," Atria Books, New York, 2017, p. 21.

Source: Gallup Poll and General Social Survey, 1972-2018.

TMIY

A Neurological Reality

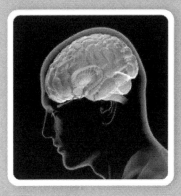

Pornography activates the brain's reward circuitry, releasing large amounts of dopamine. The brain builds a tolerance to dopamine requiring ever greater stimulation. Pornography is addictive.

Dopamine activates sexual centers in the brain's hypothalamus, which sends signals to the erectile center in the spinal cord. When the hypothalamus builds a tolerance to dopamine, it weakens the signal to the erectile centers. Pornography is associated with erectile dysfunction.

Pornography activates the mPFC, posterior cingulate and temporal lobes. Women are viewed as objects. Mentally, men are placed in a state to "use a tool."

Source: Voon, V., "Neural Correlates of Sexual Cue Reactivity in Individuals with and without Compulsive Sexual Behaviours," PLOS ONE, July 2014, v. 9, Issue 7, e102419.
Robinson, M., et al., "Cupid's Poisoned Arrow-Porn Induced Sexual Dysfunction: A Growing Problem," Psychology Today, July 11, 2011.
Cikara, M., et al., "From Agents to Objects: Sexist Attitudes and Neural Responses to Sexualized Targets," Journal of Cognitive Neuroscience, March 2011; 23(3): 540-551.

TMIY

A Shadow in the Land

Millions of humans are trapped in human trafficking each year.

79% of victims relate to sexual exploitation.

70% are women and girls.

8% are under the age of 11.

One-quarter are under the age of 17.

Almost 50% are forced to produce pornography.

The United States is a major destination for girls who are being sexually exploited.

They come from all over the world.

Source: Migration Data Portal: Human Trafficking.
Farley, M., "Renting an Organ for Ten Minutes: What Tricks Tell us about Prostitution, Pornography, and Trafficking," in Pornography: Driving the Demand for International Sex Trafficking.

TM1Y

There is always hope.

"God sent his Son into the world, not to condemn the world, but. That the world might be saved through him" (John 3:17).

"He sent me to proclaim release to the captives" (Luke 4:18).

TM1Y

TM1Y
THAT MAN IS YOU!

Session 21

- How do you prioritize faith and family in your own life?
- What actions are you doing that undermine your faith and family?
- In what ways are you helping the next generation to embrace faith and family?

Session 22

A Civilization of Love

We've crossed some difficult terrain.

We're not done yet ...

but, the light of love will be shining by the end of this session.

TMIY

An Inherent Weakness

"In place of these virtues, we have ... public need and private opulence ... we rob virtue to reward ambition. No wonder – with each one consulting his own interest, thinking only of lust at home and of fortune or favors in public life – that the republic is helpless to defend itself."

City of God v.12

"We know that communism fell in the end because of the system's socioeconomic weakness, not because it has been truly rejected as an ideology or a philosophy."

Pope St. John Paul II
Memory and Identity

Source: Augustine, "City of God," The Fathers of the Church, v. 8, The Catholic University of America Press, Washington, DC, 1950, p. 271.
Pope John Paul II, "Memory and Identity," Rizzoli, 2005, p. 48.

TMIY

Own Interest ... Private Opulence

"Our algorithms exploit the human brain's attraction to divisiveness ... if left unchecked," Facebook would feed users "more and more divisive content in an effort to gain user attention and increase time on the platform."

"The influx of competing messages ... overload our working memory. It makes it much harder for our frontal lobes to concentrate our attention on any one thing. The process of memory consolidation can't even get started ... the more we use the Web, the more we train our brain to be distracted – to process information very quickly and very efficiently, but without sustained attention."

Source: Wall Street Journal, "Facebook Executives Shut Down Efforts to Make the Site Less Divisive," May 26, 2020.
Carr, N., "The Shallows-What the Internet Is Doing to Our Brains," W.W. Norton & Company, New York, 2011, p. 194

TMIY

Public Need

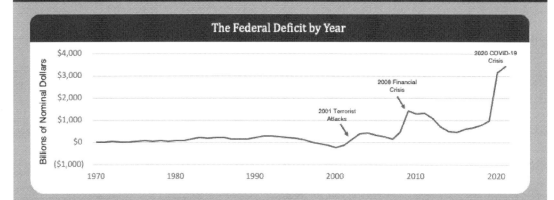

The Federal Deficit by Year

Source: Congressional Budget Office – Historical Series (1970-2020); Updated Estimate for 2021.

TMIY

Unwinding bad positions is never easy.

 "Success has many fathers, but failure is an orphan."

There has always been finger pointing.

TMIY

Unwinding the Roman Empire

"They say that this calamity has fallen upon the city of Rome because she has ceased to worship her gods ... [they] attribute the disasters which have befallen the Roman commonwealth to the fact that our religion has forbidden the offering of sacrifices to the gods."

City of God, I.15,36

"If the Tiber has overflowed its banks, if the Nile has remained in its bed, if the sky has been still, or if the earth been in commotion, if death has made its devastations, or famine its afflictions, your cry immediately is, 'This is the fault of the Christians!'"

Tertullian, Ad Nationes, I.9

Source: Augustine, "City of God," Trans. Dyson, R.W., Cambridge University Press, Cambridge, UK, 1998, p. 25 and p. 49.
Tertullian, "Ad Nationes," I.9, Ante-Nicene Fathers, v. 3, Hendrickson Publishers, Peabody, MA, 1995, p. 117.

TMIY

The Masters of Suspicion

"I raise against the Christian church the most terrible of all accusations that any accuser ever uttered... I call Christianity the one great curse... I call it the one immortal blemish on mankind."

"Religion... is the sigh of the oppressed creature, the heart of a heartless world, and the soul of soulless conditions. It is the opium of the people. The abolition of religion as the illusory happiness of the people is the demand for their real happiness."

"In Christian myth, man's original sin is undoubtedly an offense against God the Father ... [Christ] forces us to the conclusion that this sin was murder ... The religion of the son succeeds the religion of the Father. As a sign of this substitution the old totem feast is revived again in the form of communion in which the band of brothers now eats the flesh and blood of the son ... at bottom, Christian communion is ... a repetition of the crime that must be expiated."

Source: "The Portable Nietzsche," Trans. Kaufmann, W., Penguin Books, New York, 1954-1982, p. 655.
"Contribution to the Critique of Hegel's Philosophy of Right," in The Portable Marx, ed. Kamenka, E., Penguin Books, New York, 1983, p. 115.
Freud, S., "Totem and Taboo," Trans. Brill, A. A., Barnes & Noble Books, New York, 2005, pp. 145-146.

TMIY

A Modern Reality

It is estimated that one-third of the world's population suffers from religious persecution in some form, with Christians being the most persecuted group ... Evidence shows not only the geographic spread of anti-Christian persecution, but also its increasing severity. In some regions, the level and nature of persecution is arguably coming close to meeting the international definition of genocide.

-U.K. Government Report on Religious Persecution

Source: "Bishop of Truro's Independent Review for the Foreign Secretary of FCO Support for Persecuted Christians," Final Report and Recommendations, July, 2019.

TMIY

Against this backdrop, we have a calling:
Build a civilization of love.

TMIY

The Christian Commandment

 A new commandment I give to you, that you love one another; even as I have loved you, that you also love one another. By this all men will know that you are my disciples, if you have love for one another.

-John 13:34-35

TMIY

A Demanding Standard

"Jesus said, 'Father, forgive them, for they know not what they do'" (Luke 24:34).

"If any one strikes you on the right cheek, turn to him the other also" (Matthew 5:39).

"I say to you, 'Love your enemies and pray for those who persecute you, so that you may be sons of your Father in heaven'" (Matthew 5:43-44).

"They rushed together upon him. Then they cast him out of the city and stoned him ... And as they were stoning Stephen, he prayed, 'Lord Jesus, receive my spirit.' And he knelt down and cried with a loud voice, 'Lord, do not hold this sin against them'" (Acts 7:57-60).

TMIY

The Virtue of Love

"The best definition of virtue is to say it is the [right] ordering of love."

City of God xv.22

"It is not given to all men to tame their shameful lusts by Christian faith, by the grace of the Holy Spirit and out of love of Everlasting Beauty, but they do the best they can."

City of God, v.13

Source: Augustine, "City of God," The Fathers of the Church, v. 14, The Catholic University of America Press, Washington, DC, 1950, p. 469.
; Augustine, "City of God," The Fathers of the Church, v. 8, The Catholic University of America Press, Washington, DC, 1950, p. 273.

TMIY

How do we grow in virtue by right ordering love?

We go to the school of the family.

TMIY

The Call to a Familial Love

"As the Father as loved me, so have I loved you, abide in my love."

John 15:9

"Husbands, love your wives, as Christ loved the Church and gave himself up for her, that he might sanctify her … that he might present the Church to himself in splendor, without spot or wrinkle or any such thing, that she might be holy and without blemish."

Ephesians 5:25-27

TMIY

The School at Nazareth

 Nazareth is a kind of school where we may begin to discover what Christ's life was like and even to understand his Gospel... Here everything speaks to us, everything has meaning... How I would like to return to my childhood and attend the simple yet profound school that is Nazareth.

Pope St. Paul VI
Basilica of the Annunciation
January 5, 1964

A Unique Vision

Impact	Vision	Challenge
"The Western Church transformed European kinship structures during the Middle Ages and this was a key factor behind a shift to a [western] psychology."	One man, one woman in a permanent, exclusive union open to life.	• 186 of 1231 cultures dating to 8th century BC are monogamous. • 40% 1st marriages end in divorce. • ¼ of people have only had on sexual partner. • 98% use birth control at some point.

Source: Schulz, J., et al., "The Church, intensive kinship, and global psychological variation," Science 366, 707 (2019).
Ethnographic Atlas Codebook, 1998 World Cultures 10(1): 86-136.

A Civilization of Love

 The aspiration that humanity nurtures, amid countless injustices and sufferings, is the hope of a new civilization marked by freedom and peace. But for such an undertaking, a new generation of builders is needed ... You are the men and women of tomorrow. The future is in your hearts and in your hands. God is entrusting to you the task, at once difficult and uplifting, of working with him in the building of the civilization of love.

-Pope St. John Paul II
World Youth Day, Toronto, 2002

Where to begin?

"For behold, the kingdom of God is within you."

Luke 17:21

"Two loves make up these two cities: love of God [and] ... love of the world... Therefore, let each one question himself as to what he loveth: and he shall find of which he is a citizen."

Commentary Psalm 65.2

Source: Augustine, Expositions on the Book of Psalms, Nicene and Post-Nicene Fathers, First Series, v. 8, Ed. Schaff, P., Hendrickson Publishers, Peabody, MA, 1994, p. 268.

TMIY

TMIY
THAT MAN IS YOU!

Session 22

1. Where is your heart set – on the things of this world or on the things of God?
2. How does your family help you become less selfish?
3. Can you enunciate the Catholic vision of marriage and family? How well can you describe it to others?

Session 23

A Life of Dissipation

Life of Dissipation

> Father, give me the share of property that falls to me.
>
> - Luke 15:12

TMIY

Life of Dissipation

> How many of my father's hired servants have bread enough and to spare, but I perish here with hunger!
>
> –Luke 15:17

TMIY

The Conversion Process

> Father, forgive them;
> for they know not what they do.
>
> —Luke 23:34

TMIY

The Return to the Father

> Father, I have sinned against heaven and
> before you; I am no longer worthy to be
> called your son; treat me as one of your
> hired servants.
>
> —Luke 15:18-19

TMIY

The Return to the Father

> And he arose and came to his father.
>
> —Luke 15:20

TMIY

Come to Me

Come to me, all who labor and are heavy laden, and I will give you rest. Take my yoke upon you, and learn from me; for I am gentle and lowly in heart, and you will find rest for your souls.

–Matthew 11:28

TMIY

The Least of my Brethren

Truly, I say to you, as you did it to one of the least of these my brethren, you did it to me.

–Matthew 25:40

TMIY

What Will it Profit a Man

For what will it profit a man,
if he gains the whole world and forfeits his life?

–Matthew 16:26

TMIY

Strength In Christ

> I can do all things in him who strengthens me.
>
> – Philippians 4:13

TMIY

Only God

> So neither he who plants nor he who waters is anything, but only God who gives the growth.
>
> – 1 Corinthians 3:7

TMIY

TMIY THAT MAN IS YOU **Session 23**

•In your spiritual life right now, are you heading away from the Father leading a life of dissipation? Are you heading back to the Father in a spirit of conversion? Or are you kneeling at the feet of the Father receiving forgiveness and getting your marching orders for the spiritual battle ahead? What is holding you back from your spiritual progression?

•Have you ever said to yourself "There is no way God can forgive me for my sin?" In what ways does this doubt minimize the ultimate sacrifice of Jesus on the cross? Do you really think that Jesus is not waiting for you to come and reconcile with Him?

Working In Redemption

When and How to Put Atonement at the Center

TMIY

The Question of Salvation

Why does it seem like so many things in the Church are unnecessary additions?

TMIY

Participation

> Consider the practice of Israel; are not those who eat the sacrifices partners in the altar?
>
> -1 Corinthians 10:18

TMIY

Life, Death, Resurrection & Ascension

The Paschal Mystery is the life, death, resurrection and ascension of Jesus, which means that this is the foundation of the Church.

TMIY

Every Aspect of the Life of Christ

> Christ's whole earthly life - his words and deeds, his silences and sufferings, indeed his manner of being and speaking ... is a mystery of redemption.
>
> -CCC 516-517

TMIY

Partakers of the Divine Nature

> He has granted to us his precious and very great promises, that through these you ... become partakers of the divine nature.
>
> -2 Peter 1:4

TMIY

Christ Became Sin

> He made him to be sin who knew no sin, so that in him we might become the righteousness of God.
>
> -2 Corinthians 5:21

TMIY

He Took Our Nature

> Since therefore the children share in flesh and blood, he himself likewise partook of the same nature, that through death he might destroy him who has the power of death, that is, the devil.
>
> -Hebrews 2:14

TMIY

Cursed

Christ redeemed us from the curse of the law, having become a curse for us—for it is written, "Cursed be every one who hangs on a tree."

-Galatians 3:13

The Sacraments

The Sacraments apply
the finished word of Christ to us.

Baptized into His Death

Do you not know that all of us who have been baptized into Christ Jesus were baptized into his death?

-Romans 6:3

United with Him in Resurrection

For if we have been united with him in a death like his, we shall certainly be united with him in a resurrection like his.

-Romans 6:5

TMIY

Founded and Fueled

Everything in the Catholic Church is founded and fueled by the Paschal Mystery.

TMIY

TMIY Session 24
THAT MAN IS YOU

- Why do you think that so many people view the Church and the Sacraments as unnecessary additions to following Christ?

- How do you apply the Paschal Mystery of Christ to your daily life?

Session 25

The Kingdom is Like
A Great Banquet

Time to Feast!

> When it's time to fast, it's time to fast.
> When it's time to feast, it is time to
> feast.
>
> -St. Teresa of
> Avila

TMIY

Celebrate Your Faith

We have more feast days than fast
days!

TMIY

The Parable of the Great Dinner

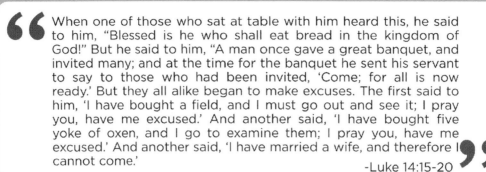

" When one of those who sat at table with him heard this, he said to him, "Blessed is he who shall eat bread in the kingdom of God!" But he said to him, "A man once gave a great banquet, and invited many; and at the time for the banquet he sent his servant to say to those who had been invited, 'Come; for all is now ready.' But they all alike began to make excuses. The first said to him, 'I have bought a field, and I must go out and see it; I pray you, have me excused.' And another said, 'I have bought five yoke of oxen, and I go to examine them; I pray you, have me excused.' And another said, 'I have married a wife, and therefore I cannot come.' "

-Luke 14:15-20

TMIY

The Parable of the Great Dinner

" So the servant came and reported this to his master. Then the householder in anger said to his servant, 'Go out quickly to the streets and lanes of the city, and bring in the poor and maimed and blind and lame.' And the servant said, 'Sir, what you commanded has been done, and still there is room.' And the master said to the servant, 'Go out to the highways and hedges, and compel people to come in, that my house may be filled. For I tell you, none of those men who were invited shall taste my banquet.' "

-Luke 14:21-24

TMIY

The Great Banquet in the Kingdom

"

Blessed are those who are invited to the marriage supper of the Lamb.

-Revelation 19:9

TMIY

TMIY

Beef Filet Tips with Brussel Sprouts and Couscous

Ingredients:

Beef
- 1 pound of beef filet tips cut into ½ inch or 1-inch pieces
- 2 Tbs olive oil
- 1 tsp salt
- ½ tsp pepper
- ½ cup panko breadcrumbs

Pan Sauce
- 2 Tbs butter
- ½-1 Tbs butter
- 1 cup red wine
- ½ -1tsp of salt
- ½ -1tsp of ground black pepper

Brussel Sprouts
- 1 Bag of Brussel sprouts (or 8-10 Sprouts, de-stemmed and halved)
- 1 Tbs olive oil
- 3 cloves garlic minced
- 1 Tbs butter
- ½ -1 tsp of salt
- 1 tsp lemon juice
- 2 Tbs Fruit jam

Couscous
- 1 Tbs butter
- 1 cup cooked couscous (cook cous cous according to instructions, drain and store)
- 4 garlic cloves minced
- 1/3 bunch parsley minced
- 1 cup cherry tomatoes halved
- ¼ cup heavy cream
- ½ -1 tsp Dash of salt
- Dash of ground black pepper

Instructions:

Beef and Pan Sauce
- In a bowl mix the beef filet tips with salt, pepper, and panko breadcrumbs.
- Put 2 Tbs of olive oil into a hot pan, once hot put the beef mixture into the pan and stir occasionally for about 2 minutes or medium rare.
- Put the beef on a plate to rest.
- Take the pan hot pan that the beef was just in and put it back over the heat, add 2 Tbs of butter to mix with the beef drippings.
- Deglaze the pan with 1 cup of red wine and reduce by half.
- Season the sauce with a dash of salt and pepper, turn off the heat, and whisk in ½ Tbs to 1 Tbs of butter to thicken the sauce.
- Add the beef back into the sauce and toss to coat it, then its ready for serving.

Brussel Sprouts
- Cut the end stem pieces off the Brussel sprouts where they were attached to the stalk, then cut them in half down the center.
- Put 1 Tbs of olive oil in a hot pan, then lay the Brussel sprouts face down in the pan and leave them like this for several minutes to get a nice sear on them.
- Add 3-4 cloves of minced garlic into the pan and stir the brussels, followed by 1 Tbs of butter.
- Add a dash of salt, 1 tsp lemon juice, and 2 Tbs fruit jam into the pan with the brussels and stir.
- Cook the brussels until they are fork tender, but they still have a bit of crunch to them (about 5 to 6 minutes total).

Couscous
- Heat up a separate pan and melt 1 Tbs of butter.
- Once melted add 4 cloves of minced garlic, 1/3 bunch of parsley minced, and 1 cup of cherry tomatoes halved.
- After a few minutes season with a dash of salt and pepper and add 1 cup of cooked couscous to the pan. Since the couscous is already cooked it wont take long, the goal is just to get it hot.
- Once the couscous is warm at ¼ cup of heavy cream and stir until incorporated and the couscous is finished.

Plating
Plate this delicious dish with a dollop of couscous in the center, top it with the saucy beef tips, and surround it with brussels. You can choose to add a bit of parsley on top for a garnish.

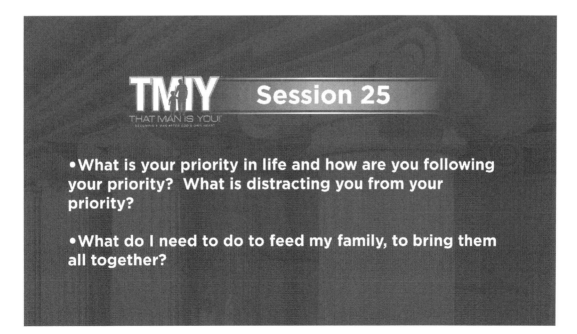

TMIY
THAT MAN IS YOU
Session 25

- **What is your priority in life and how are you following your priority? What is distracting you from your priority?**

- **What do I need to do to feed my family, to bring them all together?**

 **Session 26**

A Royal People

Altus Christus

The word "Christ" means "anointed"

 TMIY

Priest - Prophet - King

"

Just as Jesus was anointed priest, prophet and King, so may you live always as a member of his body sharing everlasting life.

-Baptism Rite

TMIY

Baptized into a New Way

> " This sacrament is also called "the washing of regeneration and renewal by the Holy Spirit," for it signifies and actually brings about the birth of water and the Spirit without which no one can enter the kingdom of God.
>
> -CCC 1215 "

Priest - Prophet - King

1	Priest - To Sanctify
2	Prophet - To Teach
3	King - To Govern and Lead

Priest

> " On entering the People of God through faith and Baptism, one receives a share in this people's unique, priestly vocation: "Christ the Lord, high priest taken from among men, has made this new people 'a kingdom of priests to God, his Father.
>
> -CCC 784 "

King

> Finally, the People of God shares in the royal office of Christ. He exercises his kingship by drawing all men to himself through his death and Resurrection. Christ, King and Lord of the universe, made himself the servant of all, for he came "not to be served but to serve, and to give his life as a ransom for many." For the Christian, "to reign is to serve him," ... The People of God fulfills its royal dignity by a life in keeping with its vocation to serve with Christ.
>
> -CCC 786

TMIY

The Royal Office

> Finally, the People of God shares in the royal office of Christ. He exercises his kingship by drawing all men to himself through his death and Resurrection. . . For the Christian, "to reign is to serve him," particularly when serving "the poor and the suffering, in whom the Church recognizes the image of her poor and suffering founder." ... The sign of the cross makes kings of all those reborn in Christ and the anointing of the Holy Spirit.
>
> -CCC 786

TMIY

Dignity and Responsibility of Our Inheritance

> For what other end do we have, if not to reach the kingdom which has no end?
>
> -St. Augustine

TMIY

You Are Anointed

> The anointing with sacred chrism, perfumed oil consecrated by the bishop, signifies the gift of the Holy Spirit to the newly baptized, who has become a Christian, that is, one "anointed" by the Holy Spirit, incorporated into Christ who is anointed priest, prophet, and king.
>
> -CCC 1241

TMIY

TMIY | **Session 26**

THAT MAN IS YOU!

• What concretely can you do to exercise your kingship and priesthood in your family?

• What does it mean for you to be a royal people, holy, set aside for the Lord? How does this impact your work and family life?

The 7 Steps of TMIY
A Spiritual Plan of Life

Develop a plan for your spiritual life as the TMIY year progresses. Fill out practical actions for each of the 7 Steps.

1. Honor your wedding vows:
-
-
-

> Starter Recommendations: Substantially reduce the use of the media, especially any with highly sexualized images or themes. Go to bed at the same time as your spouse. End the day with at least 15 minutes of conversation with your spouse.

2. Use money for others:
-
-
-

> Starter Recommendations: Substantially reduce the use of the media. Eat dinner together with your family. Use financial resources for the benefit of the family and the Church.

3. Give God some of your time:
-
-
-

> Starter Recommendations: Substantially reduce the use of the media. Pray the Rosary every day. Begin and end each day with at least 10 minutes of prayer. A morning offering and end of day examination of conscience work well.

4. Set your mind on the things above:
-
-
-

> Starter Recommendations: Read Sacred Scripture for at least 10 minutes a day. Lectio Divina is encouraged. Read a Spiritual book with your spouse or your small group. Create daily silence in your life to be attentive to the still, small voice of God.

5. Find God in yourself:
-
-
-

> Starter Recommendations: Receive Christ in the Eucharist at least once/week in addition to Sunday. Develop prayer "triggers" to keep a constant dialogue going with God throughout the day. Establish a personal relationship with the Holy Spirit.

6. Find God in other people:
-
-
-

> Starter Recommendations: Never speak in anger towards your spouse and/or children. Give your spouse compliments every day. Ask God to help you find his Hidden Face in your Spouse and Children.

7. Practice superabundant mercy (Make it easy to be good and hard to be bad):
-
-
-

> Starter Recommendations: Go to Confession once a month to experience God's mercy. Forgive those who have hurt you, starting with your spouse. Give the gift of your joyful presence within your home.

NOTES

NOTES

NOTES

NOTES

NOTES

NOTES

NOTES

Made in the USA
Columbia, SC
06 September 2021

44852170R00074